C000004087

Around Stony Stratford

IN OLD PHOTOGRAPHS

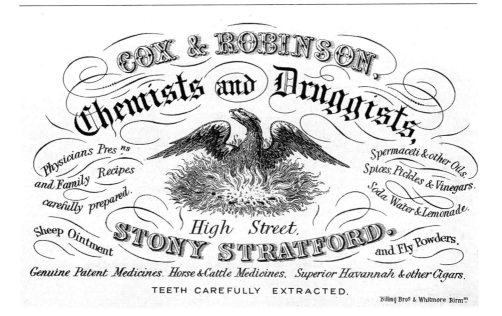

COX & ROBINSON,

Chemists and Druggists,

Physicians Pres^{ns} and Family Recipes carefully prepared.

Spermaceti & other Oils, Spices, Pickles & Vinegars. Soda Water & Lemonade.

Sheep Ointment

High Street, **STONY STRATFORD.**

and Fly Powders.

Genuine Patent Medicines. Horse & Cattle Medicines. Superior Havannah & other Cigars.

TEETH CAREFULLY EXTRACTED.

Billing Bros & Whitmore Birm^m

FURNITURE REMOVERS.

Stony Stratford, Bucks.

HOLLAND S. & SON, Vicarage road. Carmen

GOODS CAREFULLY REMOVED

S. HOLLAND & SON
VICARAGE ROAD,
STONY STRATFORD

ROAD ᴼᴿ RAIL

and contractors for the removal of furniture by road & rail. Furniture, &c., warehoused on reasonable terms.   Estimates free

Examples of Victorian business cards used by prominent tradesmen.

Around Stony Stratford

IN OLD PHOTOGRAPHS

AUDREY LAMBERT

Audrey Lambert.

Alan Sutton Publishing Limited
Phoenix Mill · Far Thrupp · Stroud
Gloucestershire

First Published 1994

Copyright © Audrey Lambert, 1994

British Library Cataloguing in Publication Data.
A catalogue record for this book is available from
the British Library.

ISBN 0 7509 0517 4

Typeset in 9/10 Sabon.
Typesetting and origination by
Alan Sutton Publishing Limited.
Printed in Great Britain by
Redwood Books, Trowbridge.

Outside the Cock Hotel, Stony Stratford. During the peak of the coaching age, from the mid-eighteenth century to the coming of the railway in 1838, some forty stagecoaches per day used Watling Street. In the inns, travellers' tales grew in the telling, hence the saying a 'cock and bull' story.

Contents

Hanslope celebrates Queen Victoria's Golden Jubilee, 1887. The banner, far centre, reads 'The Committee wish all to Eat, Drink & Be Merry'. William Ditum, wearing a bowler hat, is sitting at the end of the table on the right-hand side, nearest the camera. The pound seen on the right was dismantled when new houses were built adjacent to the site in the mid-1970s.

Introduction

The area described in this volume is geographically located both in north Buckinghamshire and south Northamptonshire; some sixteen towns and villages are illustrated here. Until quite recently the history of this 'close' area was chronicled only in separate volumes on the two counties. The area is administered by three districts, based at Central Milton Keynes, Aylesbury and Towcester.

Villages grew up in forest clearings, or as settlements alongside the Roman Watling Street catering for passing travellers. Modern Fenny Stratford is near Roman Magiovinium while Towcester is Lactodorum. It was a border area in many national struggles such as those against the Danes and later in the Civil War. The *Anglo-Saxon Chronicle* tells us that Edward the Elder encamped at Passenham in AD 921 while Towcester was being fortified. Already by the late twelfth century Stony Stratford had been established as a market-place on Watling Street: Stony Stratford West in the manor of Calverton, Stony Stratford East in Wolverton. Sadly the Eleanor Cross in Stony Stratford West, commemorating the halt there of the cortège of King Edward I's Queen Eleanor in 1290, was destroyed in the Civil War.

Traditionally hunting country, particularly in the Whaddon Chase, Whittlewood and Salcey Forests, throughout history royal visitors and hunting parties crossed the area and great men built their manor houses and mansions, notably at Whaddon, Bradwell, Loughton, Beachampton, Passenham, Calverton, Wolverton, and off the Northampton road at Grafton Regis, Alderton and Stoke Bruerne. The home of the Duke of Grafton was to be at Wakefield Lodge near Potterspury – the characteristic estate farmhouses can be recognized in many south Northamptonshire villages. The clock-maker William Knibb settled in Hanslope, near the Northamptonshire border; the lofty spire of St James's Church is a landmark from many vantage points in the area.

In the early nineteenth century the engineers of the Grand Union Canal and of the London & Birmingham Railway followed similar routes up-country bringing quicker and more economic forms of transport for both passengers and goods, thereby ending the stagecoach era on Watling Street. Numbers of workers and new inhabitants came to the area from all parts of the country. Then a century later – in 1959 – the M1 motorway opened just to the east, also initially having a great impact on traffic on Watling Street. How many can remember those pre-M1 Silverstone Grand Prix race-days when Stony Stratford High Street was lined with townsfolk watching a continuous stream of vehicles going through the town?

Agriculture and lace-making had been the staple local industries before the Industrial Revolution. With the advent of steam-power new industries developed dramatically in the nineteenth century and the landscape was altered by the construction of impressive engineering works and new roads. To Stony Stratford came Samuel Sharp the currier, while at Deanshanger was Edwin and Henry Roberts' iron foundry. Wolverton can claim to be the first 'railway town' in the country, with its associated factory, followed by a satellite development at New Bradwell. The Wolverton factory was to be transformed into a major railway carriage-building centre, and was the largest employer in the locality. In 1878 McCorquodale's Printing Works was also established there. From Wolverton a branch railway was constructed to Newport Pagnell and a narrow-gauge steam tramway to Deanshanger for the workers.

Meanwhile at Stony Stratford in the 1840s, Edward Hayes, an ex-Wolverton apprentice, established the Watling Works to manufacture agricultural machinery. Unusually on an inland site, his son later started building steam tugs and launches which were launched on the canal at the Old Stratford Wharf. In mid-century there was close cooperation between a local group of engineers: J.E. McConnell at Wolverton, Edward Hayes I at Stony Stratford, Thomas Rickett, manufacturing steam carriages at the Castle Foundry, Buckingham (in Stony Stratford in 1851), and William Smith at Little Woolstone, the agricultural inventor and innovator.

A century and a half later we find another rapidly changing scenario. Of the many Stony Stratford firms that served the town and the surrounding countryside sadly only the names of Cowley, Cox & Robinson, Franklin, Haseldine and Odell still remain while Sharp's (ex-Sharp & Woollard) has migrated to Cosgrove.

When Her Majesty the Queen and the Duke of Edinburgh visited the Wolverton UDC offices in Stony Stratford Market Square and Warren Farm, Old Wolverton, in 1966 it was known that the northern towns and surrounding villages in north Buckinghamshire were to be part of a 'new town', designed for the age of the motor-car. Since then the promotion of the Milton Keynes shopping centre, the growth of superstores and the accent on the car has affected life not only in the 22,000-acre Milton Keynes New Town development but also neighbouring villages such as Nash and Passenham where infilling and modernization of dwellings threaten to engulf their former rural character. What we knew as individual villages, farms and fields, such as Bradwell, Loughton and the Shenleys have been lost to large housing developments, although relieved by attractive areas of parkland, while even the once isolated Tattenhoe is set to lose its rural identity.

The problem of the car is particularly apparent in the older parts of the settlements which were built before its invention or subsequent great popularity. In the evening the heart of Stony Stratford is full of cars; Wolverton has a row of car showrooms on the main road, and its streets seem to be full of 'sleeping policemen' to slow traffic. Conversely, in Northamptonshire, Deanshanger and Yardley Gobion are bypassed and Wicken is effectively now 'off the beaten track'.

This feverish activity contrasts firmly with the atmosphere of the photographs that Audrey Lambert has selected and meticulously researched from the archives of so many willing contributors. She reminds us of the lives of 'ordinary' people, displaying their strong community spirit. I recall Mr Thorneycroft taking the photograph of St Giles' Church choir, Stony Stratford. Elsewhere my great-grandfather, who came from Totternhoe in 1872, proudly tries out his brother-in-law's car. My father's two sisters, stalwarts of the Women's Institute, assist at an old people's party. Bill Beeton, shown driving through floods in the 1930s, drove us to school in the late 1940s.

We owe a debt of heartfelt gratitude to the family and professional photographers whose work is published here for posterity. Audrey Lambert has shown those of us 'Around Stony Stratford' that we have a proud tradition to uphold.

Robert Ayers
Local Historian
Vice President, Wolverton & District Archaeological Society
1994

SECTION ONE

Stony Stratford

'Top of the Town.' Peter Brazell cycles past the Plough Inn, formerly St Mary's Church School, built in 1873. Note the old finger-post and the sunblinds over the shops at the entrance to the High Street.

A step back in time to a shop established in 1760. Carved and scalloped bottle 'runs', a leech jar, bloodletting knives, instruments for drawing teeth and fine tobacco jars can be seen behind the Georgian front. The last owner, from 1946 to 1979, was Mr W.P.B. Phillpotts.

An early car, probably a Panhard, outside No. 3 Vicarage Road, c. 1910. The occupants are Samuel Holland and his wife Jane (née Johnson), his daughter Kate, his son George, Arthur Johnson jnr and Edith Betts. Samuel's firm were also coal merchants and general railway and cartage agents.

'To live long, live at Stony Stratford.' Mr C.P. Woollard JP, having compiled a record of elderly residents, arranged a reunion in August 1927 during which the aged men were photographed at the entrance to The Retreat. One group of ten had an average age of just under 84 years and this group of twenty-four an average age of about 80 years. Back row, left to right: -?-, George Faulkner (76), Reuben Tucker (76), Robert French (77), Charles Smith (82), James Tingey (77), Britton Harris (76), George Benson (78), John Marsh (76), -?-. Middle row: -?-, Frank Loveless (75), William Baldwin (86), -?-, Thomas J. Calladine (84), Thomas Kirby (85), -?-. Front row: -?-, William Hull (87), James Dillow (84), Walter J. Crisp (88), Richard Matthews (85), Charles Johnson (84), James Betts (82). Also in the photograph are Ted Smith (80), George Taylor (78) and a few others, not identified. Mr William Lever snr (78), and Mr Dan Cowley (83) were unable to be present, the latter through being on business! Afterwards Mr Woollard entertained his guests to a meat tea in the Public Hall.

Herbert Cecil Holland in the doorway of his Midland Furnishing Stores, at No. 3 Market Square, *c.* 1911. Holland, a cabinet maker and upholsterer, specialized in genuine antique and new furniture, and household ironmongery. The business closed during the First World War.

Standing in front of the cart are Jonathan and Ada Haseldine, with their son Tom and daughter Violet. Their bakery business was founded in 1871 by Jonathan's father George. Tom's son John and his grandson Richard now trade from Nos 23 & 73 High Street.

The first bread vehicle: Hugh Cowley with Taffy, *c.* 1900. Hugh's father, Daniel, a cricketer for Bucks County, was landlord of the Bull Hotel, and later a baker at 16 Market Square.

A familiar and welcome sight: Arthur Cowley with Bill passing the Old School, Calverton, on his delivery round, *c.* 1950s. In 1961 the iron-tyred wheels on the hundred-year-old cart (formerly belonging to a bootmaker) broke, and deliveries by van took over!

Harry Joseph Brazell was born at Quainton. A rural postman, his route was from Stony Stratford to Castlethorpe; he left at 10.50 a.m. going via Cosgrove village and post office at 11.30 a.m., arriving at 12.30 p.m. He then returned at 1 p.m. via Castlethorpe Wharf, Cosgrove post office and Old Stratford, arriving at 2.30 p.m. The walking distance was 9 miles 4 furlongs, for which he was paid 21s 6d weekly. He was awarded the Imperial Service Medal on 13 September 1929 for 'meritorious services'.

Standing proudly outside the just completed post office are Thomas Betts (extreme right), painter, glazier, decorator and builder, and his workmen. This postcard is dated 1906.

The construction of Nos 35, 33, and 31 Clarence Road, *c.* 1920s. Jubilee Terrace is visible on the left. Left to right: John Franklin, -?-, -?-, -?-, -?-, 'Bowey' Ratcliffe, Sam Tarry, -?-. George Franklin from Thornborough established the firm, building the town fire station in 1864. The present owners, Walter and his son John Franklin, are the third and fourth generations in the firm.

The new sewerage system being laid on The Green, 1905. The entrance to the Baptist Church can be seen on the left.

Tannery workers applying currier's dubbin to almost finished leather, c. 1974. Bill Swain (nearest camera), a native of Cosgrove, joined Sharp & Woollard from school and completed over fifty years' service, for some years as foreman. Les Pulley, Stony Stratford born and bred, also retired from the company after many years' service. The business dates back to the seventeenth century when a tanyard was established by the Penn family. The earliest surviving document, on parchment, is dated 1730. Samuel Sharp came from Towcester in 1819 and purchased the business in Church Street. He was joined in 1845 by Mr F.W. Woollard, a young man from London, the firm then taking the name Sharp & Woollard. In 1873 the company was awarded a medal for its saddlery leather at the first Leather Trade's Exhibition held at Northampton. (This was later transferred to London to become the National Exhibition.) The Church Street premises closed in 1990 by which time production had been transferred to the Cosgrove factory opened in 1984 as Samuel Sharp (Curriers) Ltd. The company enjoys a high reputation for its saddlery leather, about 70 per cent of which is now exported. The largest market is India. Others are Japan, Australia, New Zealand, USA, Scandinavia and most European countries. In 1991 the company received an Enterprise Development Award for Exports from the Department of Trade and Industry. Mr Peter Brazell and his brother Norman are now the joint owners.

Percy Westley, here posing with his first vehicle, started his carrier's business in 1929. Operating around the district and as far as Northampton, he would carry almost anything in the days before mass car-ownership. His son, Eric, continued to manage the removals and storage business in which he worked for twenty-nine years.

The last shoeing smith at work: Rupert Roberts at his forge, now demolished, in Church Street, c. 1950. He is shoeing Smiler (a biter!) for Bob Webb of Calverton. (Photo loaned by Bob's son, John Webb.)

One of the last Hayes boats, *Pat* was built for Beckett's of Kingston and used for many years on the Thames. Here it is being transported by steam lorry past Lloyds Bank, High Street, to Old Stratford for its launch in the canal basin around 1925. Edward Hayes started Watling Works around 1847, manufacturing farm machinery and later steam launches, tugs and yachts which were exported around the world. His son and grandson were both named Edward. The last named died in 1920.

John Cooper and his wife Sarah (née Lovell) outside their home in King Street, *c.* 1910. He was a painter and decorator, second of three generations in the trade.

Mrs Sibthorpe outside Pollard's shop, *c*. 1930. Her brothers, Will and Jim Pollard, ran Pollard Bros, tailors to the gentry, including hunt people, specializing in breeches. This business closed in 1934. Mr J.T. Barnes opened Barnes Restaurant on the site in 1937, and his son, Brian, retired on Christmas Eve, 1987.

Floods at the north end of High Street were once a common sight. The houses were regularly swamped. Bill Beeton is at the wheel of the Eastern National Leyland Lion LT2 32-seater bus, believed to be No. 2996, TM 6309, built in 1930.

The oldest business in the town was established in 1763. This photograph, of around 1894, shows James Odell and wife Ellen (formerly a Miss Selby of Wormleighton, Warks) and their family. Back, left to right: Frank, Ella, Allan, May, Leo, Amy, Victor. Centre: James, Ellen, Faith. Front: Muriel, Daisy. Having purchased the ironmonger's business at 60/62, High Street, from the owner Edwin Revell, James began trading in 1863. In the 1881 census he was described as a 'master ironmonger', employing six men. He advertised '"Unrivalled" Horse or Turnip Hoes, Scarifiers & Grubbers'. Of his children, May became housekeeper to Mr James Maclean, Pharmacist of Cox & Robinson, and lived to be over ninety years of age; Muriel married W.J. Higgs, for many years a butcher in Market Square, and Lionel (Leo) who married Bessie Sulston, became Managing Director of Odell & Co. Ltd. His twin sons Lionel and Ronald and their sister Audrey all went into the business. Ronald built up an extensive collection of antique ironmongery and regularly exhibited in the town's library; one display was of 'candlesticks and rushlight holders of the past 200 years'. Audrey still plays an active part in the shop which is now run by Ronald's two sons, Richard and David.

Formed in the 1860s, the Stony Stratford Band played in the Market Square for King Edward VII's Coronation on 9 August 1902, and was prominent before 1914 at carnivals and fêtes. This photograph was taken outside St Giles' Parish Room. In the centre is Mr Woollard (with silk hat), on his right is Dr W.H. Bull and on his left is Mr John Cooper. The band was wound up in 1929.

Mr W.W. (Billy) Dickens, a local benefactor. Born at Nash, he was one of thirteen children. From a smallholding in Old Stratford, he eventually owned three farms (totalling 500 acres), and a hundred houses. He was well known at sheep fairs in the country and owned a corn-merchant shop in the High Street (now Jardines). He was interviewed by the local press on his ninetieth birthday, on 11 September 1959, by which time he had given away sums of money to many churches and other organizations in the district.

MR. W. W. DICKENS,
County Council Candidate.

The Rogers family in front of the watermill at Mill Field. Standing, left to right: Robin, Miriam, Alfred, James, Kathleen, Douglas Milne-Smith, Randolph. Sitting: Flora, Elizabeth (née Roads of Norduck), Mary. Robin married Miriam Cowley of Stony Stratford in 1912, and farmed at Chackmore. Miriam lived at St Denys in the Market Square. Alfred farmed at Beachampton. Kathleen married Douglas Milne-Smith. Mary married Frank Chennells of Passenham in 1915 and lived at Eshowe in Zululand. James Rogers was born at Cogenhoe in 1836. His father, Robert, moved with his large family to Buckingham in 1855. They worked in the mills and also farmed. At one time the Rogers family owned all the mills between Buckingham and Stony Stratford. James lived at Tyrellcote for a year or so while Stony Stratford Mill and house were built or altered. He was at Stony Stratford Mill 1871–1916 and was succeeded by Mr A.E. Catt. The mill was still working in the 1920s but was demolished around 1988 after a fatal fire in the converted factory unit building.

The mill race and wheel photographed by Sylvia Clarke with a Brownie camera, *c*. 1938. This part of the River Ouse was one of the most pleasant stretches of water in the district.

Skating on Mill Field during a severe winter in the nineteenth century. During the winter of 1870 it was possible to skate from the basin terminus of the Buckingham branch of the Grand Union Canal all the way to Old Stratford.

Boys from St Giles' School at the Barley Mow bathing place, *c.* 1928. Back row, left to right: Bert Tucker, ? Daniels, Ivor Johnson, Bert Savage, Dougie Higgs, Claude Bailey, Ken Sawford, -?-, Allen Holland (tall boy, centre), -?-, ? James, Jim Taylor, -?-, George Shurmer, Nelson Grace, -?-, -?-, Michael Green. Middle row, fifth from left: Bob Caudle; sixth from left; ? Davis; tenth from left: Eric Stevens; twelfth from left: Tom Fensome; thirteenth from left: Jacky Cohen. Front row, second from left: Basil Wilmin; third from left: ? Brown; fifth from left: ? James.

Proudly posing for the camera, the boys of St Giles' School won the School Cup in 1902, the first time the cup had been competed for by the four Stony Stratford schools. They won it again in 1903 and 1904. Back row, left to right: Mr O. Baldock (Headmaster), Reggie Betts, Reg Shouler, Revd Mr Last, R. Claridge, Jim Frost, D. Meakins (Assistant Master), Wilf Lines, Eddie Foulks. Front row: Jimmy Castle (with long trousers), Dave Goodridge, Cyril Gillard, Jack Goodridge (Captain), Rupert Meadows and Charlie Herbert.

St Giles' C. of E. Boys' School, Standard 3, 1928. Back row, left to right: Jack Goodridge, Fred Alderman, Wilf Sims, Roy Elson, Cyril Roberts, Fred Rowley. Middle row: Reg Westley, Ernie Stewart, Joe Caudle, Stafford Johnson, Alfred Wilmin. Front row: Lesley Rowley, Jim Taberner, Willie Brown, Aubrey Bishop, Frank Eaton, Alfred Jackson, Tom Fensom, Alfred Cox, Philip Wilmin, Jack Anderson and Kenneth Holman. Note the canister on the wall to measure rainfall.

In the orchard, pupils of the Nursery School, c. 1940s. Back row, left to right: Robert Frisby, Vicky Mallows, Graham Deal, Trevor Read, Mrs Gladys Cropper, Roy Savage, Olive Saving, Norman Wigley. Middle: Mavis Brown, Dorothy Reeday, David Fensom, Robert West, Pauline Pulley, Diane Beechey, -?-, Jane Fisher, David Carter, Robert Valentine, Lorraine Smith. Front: Caroline Whitlock, Gwen Foote, Pam Holland.

Pupils from Russell Street School, 1923. This Council School opened in 1907. Back row, left to right: George Gunthorpe, -?-, Stella Holman, Blossom Harwood, Amy Russell, Rose Fidler, Dorothy Beeton, Reg Grace, Cyril Connor. Second row: Bill Chapman, Bert Hooton, Fred Richardson, Ken Green, Ken Dillow, -?-, Ron Stevens. Third row: Hilda Smith, Nellie Sayers, Martha Manders, Olive Smith, Lilly Neale, Winifred Knibbs, Emily Kimble, Mary Buswell. Front row: Edie Bull, Vi Buswell, Gladys Wrighton, Phyllis Dunckley.

Pupils from the Primary School, Russell Street, with their teacher, Mrs Barker, *c.* 1959. Back row, left to right: David Dillow, Tony Lawrence, -?-, Eric Burgess, Fred Frisby, Keith Brown, Richard Haseldine, -?-, David Daniell, Brian Fossey, Robert Justice. Middle row: -?-, Paul Holbrook, Martin Pettifer, Ian Henson, Brian Simms, -?-, Christine Temple, Lesley Ratcliffe, Vi Wise, -?-, Hilary Reid, -?-. Front row: -?-, Yvonne Savage, Elizabeth Walker, -?-, Sue Partridge, Ruth Gilles, Delia Forman, Elizabeth Temple.

A class from the Primary School, photographed on 10 November 1949. Back row, left to right: Mrs Hamilton, -?-, John Crouch, Roy Trimmer, Elizabeth Richardson, Gordon Sargent, Rodney Whitehead, Anne Rowledge, David Weatherhead, Ronald Best, Ron Jones, Barbara Dickens, Miss Clysdale. Middle row: Ann Mitchell, Janet Buswell, Celia Baud, Joan Young, Jennifer Smith, John Frisby, Ann Chipperfield, -?-, Brian Andrews, Ian James, Barbara Frost, Moira Clarke. Front row: Colin Wrightson, Edna Colborne, John Robinson, John Andrews, Ann Barley, -?-, Oswald Tee, Dorothy Brown, Bernard Foote, Linda Barley.

Stony Stratford Church Senior School, built by Betts and Faulkner, was completed in 1937. It was later renamed St Mary and St Giles Church of England Middle School. When the new school opened, its headmaster was Mr W. Toms. He was headmaster of St Giles' School when it closed, and the organist at St Giles' Church for many years. This photo was taken in 1941. Back row, left to right: Les Smith, Peter Green, Eric Tutt, Colin Willett, Brian Edwards, Bob Goldney, David Jones, -?-, Brian Holman. Second row: Phyllis Wood, Rosemary Grace, Lily Knight, June Richardson, Eileen Glenn, Sylvia Noble, Pat Ward, Alma Bull. Third row: Mr Rufus Owen, Derek Bowden, Douglas Dormer, Austin Robinson, -?-, Brian Tompkins, John Green, Michael Parker, Trevor White, Ken Shean, Mr Billy Toms (Headmaster). Front row: Sheila Lake, Beryl Wilson, Angela Kingston, Doreen Mills, Janet Richardson, Joyce Hanwell, Dorothy Onan, Stella Farmer, Brenda Tapp, Sheila West. The Archbishop of York, Dr John Habgood, took part in the school's Golden Jubilee celebrations in 1987. Dr Habgood was brought up in the area, and his father was a local doctor. Also present was the Lord Lieutenant, John Freemantle, whose grandfather was present at the opening of the school.

St Giles' and St Mary's Senior School netball team, 1946/7. Back row, left to right: Margaret Barden, Joyce Cotton, Thelma Robinson. Middle row: Margaret Nicholls, Ann Marks, Kathleen ?, Barbara Downing, Betty Shurmer. Front row: Pam Wheeler, Nina Eales, Sylvia Benbow, Dawn Rollings, Peggy Hanwell, Diane Eglesfield, Barbara Turner.

Enjoying a race in their pedal-cars are Dorothea Bailey and her cousin Leslie Aylott, on the pavement outside their homes in Clarence Road, *c.* 1930s. Note the railings which were commandeered for the war effort in the Second World War.

Photographed on the circular entrance drive to York House School in London Road are the pupils with the Principal, Mrs Adelaide Slade and her two daughters, *c.* 1922. Back row, left to right: Elizabeth Weston, Nancy Bosworth, Mary Payne, Mary Crofts, -?-, Emily Lennox, Marjorie Barnard, -?-, Doris Fordham. Second row: Miss Geraldine Butler, Miss Lorna Hartogg, Miss Flossie Key, Miss Janet McAlister, Miss Helen Hollier (all teachers), Monica Chandler, Phyllis Russell, Frances Insley, Dorothy Davis, -?-, Georgina Russell, Phyllis Howes, Audrey Insley, Violet Barwood, Noelle Dell, Hilda Greenwood, Phyllis Wicks, Edith Oldham, Queenie Young, Emily Faulkner. Third row: Joan Meakins, Dorothy Meadows, Doreen Sawbridge, Kathleen Coop, Sylvia Arkwright, Lucy Scott, Kitty Johnson, Dorothy Schooler, Margaret Smith, Gussie Norman, Peggy Fordham, Sybil Wheelden, Phyllis Meacham. Fourth row: Miss Agnes Slade, Bea Marshall, Marjorie Hobbs, Mollie Watson, Elsie Broom, Connie Holes, Mabel Dormer, Eva Towersey, -?-, -?-, Marjorie Clewett, Ivy Pratt, Ethel Thompson, Marjorie Meakins, Beatrice Downing, Ethel Thompson, Mary Sansom (housekeeper), Miss Dorothy Slade. Fifth row: Edna Holland, Amy Harkness, Aggie Barley, Dorothy Styles, Betty Pryke, Phoebe Downing, Vera Hargreaves, Mrs Adelaide Slade, May Bright, Linda Cockerill, Eileen Brett, Gladys Holland, Lily Allen, Betty Davis, Joyce Brett, Jean Smith. Sixth row: Edith Valentine, Margaret Cheshire, Clarice Tailby, Judy Amphlett, Dora Mackerness, Peggy Tibbetts, Edna Sawbridge, Dorothy Moss, Sydney Croxon, Claire Cockerill, Mary Moss, Kathleen Fairburn, Eileen ('Bobbie') Higgs, Stephanie Meacham, Audrey Odell. Front row: Jim Mortimer, Clifton Smith, Jack Weston, Jack Adams, Gerald Langley, John Mortimer, Peter Phillpotts, Dora Baxter, Peggy Barr. The school was opened by Mrs Slade at her home in Hanslope in 1853. After several moves, and after the death of the founder, her daughter-in-law, Mrs Edward Slade continued to run the school at York House (now the Conservative Club) before finally moving to Clarence House in London Road. The prospectus described York House as standing on high ground on the outskirts of the town, in a particularly healthy situation! In the 1930s fees for pupils over twelve years old were £6 6s per term for day pupils and 25 guineas per term for boarders. Miss Marjorie Ogilvie took over as Principal on the retirement of the Misses Slade in 1933 and the school continued until its closure in 1957. It is now the York House Youth Club.

The Greek dancing group at York House School, 1937. Back row, left to right: J. Wood, M. Gardener, Joy Gerrard (on top of fountain), B. Dyke, R. West. Second row, from extreme left: Jean Turney, B. Mortimer, Joan Gardener, Rosemary Woollard, J. Joyce, Sheila Slight, Rosemary Faulkner (on fountain), R. Mortimer, Kathleen Anstee, -?-, Nellie Robinson, Irene Andrews, Beryl Cobley (extreme right). Third row: Jean Andrews, M. Hurst, Ann Slight, June Wilkes, Betty Thompson. Front row: Ruth Whiting, J. Thompson, A Morton, Claire Robinson, Ruth Ogilvie, -?-.

A delightful chorus line from the Gwendolyn Randall Dancing Troupe, entertaining at one of their many charity performances, *c.* 1948. Left to right: ? Swann, Pat Cook, Dorothy Brown, Ann Underwood, Edna Colborne, Doreen Sims, Dylis Drinkwater, Mary Simpson, -?-, ? Andrews, Anne Colborne.

Frances Shean sent this postcard to a friend named Lily, *c.* 1908. 'I am sending you a post card of myself and hope you will like it.' She writes that her two friends are Florrie Timms and Lizzie Cox, and they are making 'Bucks Pillowlace'.

Some members of the tennis club at the bottom of Vicarage Road taking a break, c. 1940s. Back row, left to right: Dick Saunders, Mr Woodhams, Keith Wilyman.
Front row: Louie Saunders, Mrs Woodhams, Mary Knight (later Mrs Jones).

After the Executive Match (District v. County) held at Newport Pagnell Bowls Club, c. 1943. Back row, left to right: -?-, *Charlie West, Newport Pagnell player, Reg Tompkins (Olney), Olney player. Front row: *Reg Tooley, *Bill Rowledge, -?-, Wolverton player, Newport Pagnell player.
* Members of Stony Stratford Bowls Club.

There are two sets of three brothers – the Smiths and the Clarkes – in this team from Stony Stratford Sports posing for the camera, *c.* 1937. Back row, left to right: two linesmen (unknown), Les Smith, Doug Smith, Harold Smith, Gerald ('Spear') Pittam (goalkeeper), Harold Clarke, Bill ('Nobby') Clark, Percy Bardell (Trainer). Front row: Reg Westley, Frank Eaton, Tommy Clarke, Cyril Robinson, Harry Clarke.

A luncheon for 'old age pensioners' was held in Regent Hall to celebrate King George V's Silver Jubilee on 6 May 1935. Centre, back: Mr Henry Hale. Front, left to right: Mrs Taylor, Mrs Colton, Mrs Tysoe, Ruth Tooley, Jack Tooley, Mr Meakins, Mrs Meakins, Mrs Robinson, -?-. By left wall: Tom Smith, Mrs Berry, Lotte Lucas, Mrs Knibbs. By right wall: Mrs Pulley, Mrs Harry Tooley, Mrs Mackerness, Mr C. Woollard.

A street party was held in Queen Street for George VI's Coronation on 12 May 1937. On the left: Mrs and Mr Smith, Mrs Valentine, Terry Valentine, Mr 'Barney' Valentine, Mrs Fidler. On the right: Mr Allen, Miss Dobson, Mrs Langley, baby, George Langley, -?-, Joe Packer (in bowler hat), Dennis Lovell, Ruth Lovell.

Residents of Clarence Road ready to march through the street to celebrate the Coronation of Queen Elizabeth II on 2 June 1953, photographed by Bert Daniels. Centre: Bert Bennett. Right: Alan Rose.

The Women's Institute gave a Christmas party for the 'over 70s' in St Giles' and St Mary's School in the 1950s. The WI members by the far wall are, left to right: Hilda Valentine, Mrs Lake, Mrs Roberts, Mrs Harold Swain, Mrs Daniell, Mrs Grace, Alice Abbott, Mrs Mabel Read, Audrey Beardmore, Kate Sibthorp, Mrs Bessie Odell, Gladys Clark, Mrs Jimmy Knight, Mrs Tom Dumbleton. Seated at the left-hand table, far side: Mrs Calladine, -?-, Harry Grace, Mr and Mrs Tompkins, -?-, Bertha Wrighton, Joe Wrighton, -?-, Mr Johnson, -?-, -?-, -?-, -?-, Mr Holyoake, Mrs Holyoake, -?-, -?-, Jimmy Betts. Nearside: Mrs Fensom, Harry Fensom, -?-, -?-, -?-, Mrs Jones, -?-, Mrs Frost. Seated at the right-hand table, far side: -?-, Sid Higgs, Mr Lovell, Mrs Stewart, Walter Holland, Kate Holland.

'Charity Lane' was held annually on the first Saturday in June, from around 1956 to 1974, in aid of Renny Lodge Hospital and other causes. It incorporated a Flower Show and here Phyllis Danforth (née Tyler) is presenting the Edgar Tyler Rose Bowl to Jack Wilson for Best Exhibit, September 1963. In the centre is Aubrey Barby, 'mine host' of the White Horse Inn for forty years.

A welcome drink! Standing at the bar of the Workmen's Social Club, in the 1950s, are, left to right: Ken Fossey, Willie Adams, Joe Davey, Eddie Cooper, Fred Giddings, Claude Bailey, ? Grey, Norman Stephenson, George Langley.

Members of Buckingham Conservative Association, Stony Stratford Women's Branch, visited the House of Commons with their MP Major Sir Frank Markham, *c.* 1950. Back row, left to right: Mrs Woodman, Mrs Rudd, Mrs Bird, -?-, Gladys Clark, Nancy Colborne, -?-, Julie Franklin, Joan Pell, Elsie Tucker, -?-, Mrs Mackerness, Kitty Barlow, -?-, Mrs Tombs, -?-, -?-, Sir Frank Markham MP, Mrs Gammage, Daisy Hurst, Mrs Richardson, -?-, -?-, -?-, -?-, -?-, -?-. Front row: Mrs Brumwell, Mrs Sibthorp, Miss Miriam Rogers, Mary Taylor, -?-, Lottie Lucas, Lil Foulks, -?-, -?-, -?-, Miss Taylor.

The men of the Stony Stratford Auxiliary Fire Service with their Green Goddess fire engine in Vicarage Road, *c.* 1946. Back row, left to right: Ro Kightley, Stan Cockerill, Len Barby, Bert Holland, David Yates, Bernard Berry. Seated, left to right: Bill Young, Les Braggins (Station Officer), Doug Chipperfield (Leading Fireman). The fire engine needed a crew of five, including the driver who also acted as the pump man. In 1964, almost a hundred years after the people of the district contributed towards the cost of a fire engine and a station to house it, following a disastrous fire in the town, former members of the volunteer brigade watched ex-fire chief Arthur Yates unveil a plaque on the then library wall, commemorating the many years the building served the community as a fire station. Mr Yates then explained that his father had joined the brigade in 1893, and there had been a Yates in the ranks until the station closed in 1958.

During the Second World War these men formed the local Royal Observer Corps, based at Post N2, Group 12 (Stony Stratford). Their post, complete with radio room and living quarters, was at Old Stratford in the Black Horse field. These posts were positioned at 5-mile intervals to track and identify incoming aircraft, passing on details of their position and course, and so on. Back row, left to right: G.F. Hyland, F.G. Knight, L. Faulkner, S.G. Allen, H.C. Clarke, J.C. Weston, A.J. Dormer. Middle row: E.G. Taylor, F.W. Beckett, P.C. Phillpotts, S.W. Roberts (Chief Observer), F. Brazell (Leading Observer), H.S. Bailey, J.M. Knighton. Front row: H. Wildman, C. Hotson, F. Marks, C.T.B. Lawson, B. Toms.

A merry pack of Wolf Cubs: the 2nd Stony Stratford pack had just won the District Sports Trophy. They were photographed in June 1950 in Vicarage Road near their meeting place, a loft above garages in the Cock Hotel yard (now M.K. City Glaziers). Back row, left to right: Malcolm Swain, David Hall, David Wise, John Savage, Geoffrey Pallitt. Second row: Barry Miller, John Quinn, Trevor Roberts, John Tapp, Keith Bailey. Third row: Bill Clewitt, Robin Coles, Gordon Bradshaw, John Frisby, Audrey Waine (Acting Cubmaster), Gordon Reid, Terry Pickers, Colin Wrightson, John Roberts, Billy Bowker. Front row: Roger Benn, Graham Roberts, Richard White (holding shield), Michael Gedge, Alan Griffiths.

Sporting the original Baden-Powell Scout hats are the boys of the 1st Stony Stratford Boy Scouts with the group's Wolf Cubs, *c.* 1932. Their leader, Mr Tommy Dicks, was awarded the Medal of Merit for his services to scouting. His son George was the first Wolf Cub in Stony Stratford and went camping with the Scouts, travelling on the top of the kit on the trek-cart! Back row, left to right (Scouts): -?-, Edgar Henson, Frank Eaton, Fred Eaton, Joe Pritchard, Algie Forder (ACM), Wilf Clark (CM), Tom Clarke, Frank Rice, Bertie Savage, Len Forder, -?-, Reg Westley (left), Bill Crossman (right). Centre: Tom Dicks (Scoutmaster). Middle row, kneeling: Dicky Birkett, 'Sam' Savage, Ern Buswell, ? Smith, ? Welch, ? Roberts, Ray Downing, Bill Whitehead, -?-, Ron Dicks. Front row, sitting: Jack Birkett, Charlie Sharman, George Green, Ken Edwards, Cyril Robinson, Cyril Westley, Jimmy Pearson, Jack Edwards, Ben Bull.

Reunion dinners were held annually by the 1st Stony Stratford Scout Group in their scout hall, which was opened in 1937. Reunions started in the early 1950s, so this is probably one of the first. The last was held around 1966. Lady serving on extreme left: Mrs Lotte Lucas. Left-hand table, far side: S. Westley, Bill Oxby, Stan Cockerill, Archie Buswell, Alf Buswell, Ernie Buswell, George Rollings, -?-, Doug Hepworth, George Dicks, Don Rivers (at far end); near side: Les Sims, Ted Wyatt, Pete Green, Les Braggins, Ted Goodman, Sid Newman, Doug Emerton, George Wilson, Stan Richardson, -?-, Jack Batrick, -?-. Right-hand table, left side: Les Parker, Sid Davis, George Green, Ron Summers, J. Reid, -?-, Reg Whiting, Jack Pacey, -?-, -?-, Tom Underhill, -?-, -?-; right side: -?-, -?-, Fred Stanton, Bill Daniell, -?-, -?-, David Yates, Ken Ward, Graham Yates.

Some of the congregation at the last service held in the Orphanage Chapel of Mr Fegan's Homes prior to its being sold, 1961. From left to right: Mrs Linden, Mr Hollyoake, Fegan's boy, Mr Moore (Superintendent), Mrs Hollyoake, Mr Brumwell, Miss Lane, Mrs Brumwell, Mrs Kingsley, Mrs Williamson, Mr John Williamson (Chief Superintendent, Northampton, shaking hands with Mr Marriott of Little Horwood), Mrs Scarlett, Miss Basketfield, Walter Linden, Mrs Marriott, Mr Norman Bennett (ex-Superintendent), Sister Lily Scarlett (Deaconess), Mr Shillingford, Lily Sharp, Miss Alice Brazell, Syd Sharp, Mrs Bennett, Harry Kimble. Services were then held in the Mission Hall for a period. It had previously been Sammy Sayers' tinsmith's shop and is now a private house.

The pageant 'Children through the Centuries' was held at Wolverton on 5 July 1928 in aid of the Waifs and Strays Society. Back row, left to right: Bill Page, George Webb snr, George Webb jnr, -?-, Arthur Pittam, Francis Dewick, Peter Phillpotts, Bobby Higgs. Middle row: Molly Sharpe, Nancy MacPherson, Mrs Habgood, -?-, Canon E.A. Steer, Bill Read, Dr A.H. Habgood, Mary Payne, Daphne MacPherson. Front row, standing: Tony Gouch, Suzanne Gouch, Muriel Stilton, Mary Stilton.

ABC's outside broadcast cameras went to St Giles' Parish Church on 18 August 1963 for sung Eucharist. In the centre stands the Vicar, the Revd C.L.G. Hutchings, Rural Dean, with his servers Larry Francis (foreground) and Norman Beechey.

The choir of St Giles' Church, 1946–7. Back row, left to right: Arthur Webb, George Webb snr (choirmaster), George Webb jnr, Bill Clark. Extreme left: Trevor Brown. Extreme right: Tom Trasler. Second row: Cyril Brown, Bernard Tapp, Billy Eales, Billy Toms (organist), Charlie Gear, Brian Aries. Third row: Alan Haycock, Bob Ayers, John Eales, Ian Davey, Roger Tapp, John Green, John Giles. Front row: John Savage, Clive Bradshaw, David Lester, Robin Millward, Canon E.A. Steer (Vicar), Gordon Bradshaw, Billy Barby, Michael Stevens, Keith Henson. This church is one of many dedicated to the patron saint of beggars and cripples. They were often built on the main road through a town, in this case Watling Street. It was rebuilt in 1776, except for the tower, which holds a ring of eight bells. With the closure of St Mary's Church in 1968, it was re-dedicated St Mary and St Giles', and Canon C.H.J. Cavell-Northam has been the incumbent from then to the present time. Mr Derek Savage has been the organist for the past thirty-five years.

The oldest known photograph of St Giles' tower and handbell ringers, 1886. Left to right: G. Valentine, W. May, W. Robinson, W. Wooding, J. Morris, E. Yates, A. Clarke, W. Cowley.

Bellringers of St Giles', 1947. Back row, left to right: A.W. Dillow, H.E. Tompkins, W.G. Clark, J.H. Chance, A.J. Hurst, E.A. Yates. Front row: H.C. Edwards, E. Yates, T. Trasler, E.C. Lambert. Mr Edwin Yates appears in both photographs which span sixty-one years. In fact he was a ringer for seventy years and foreman for thirty-five years.

Part of the chancel screen which was destroyed in a disastrous fire in St Giles' Church on Boxing Day 1964. The fire also destroyed the hundred-year-old organ and all the photographic records in the vestry, and damaged plaster and paintwork throughout the building.

Cleaning the chancel after the fire. Left to right: Joan Brown, Evelyn Chapman, Audrey Cooper, Janet Chapman, Alice Eales.

A confirmation group photographed outside St Mary the Virgin Church, 13 November 1955. Back row, left to right: Mr Richard Franklin, Michael Stevens, Bill Clewitt, -?-, Colin Croxall, Arnold Croxall, Oswald Tee, Robin Coles, Clive Nash, -?-, Peter Rainbow, Royston Wheeler, -?-, -?-, Philip Clewitt, -?-. Second row: -?-, David Best, Yvonne Fensom, Anne Rowledge, Ann Foddy, Stewart Smith, Graham Roberts, Graham Augsberger. Front row: -?-, -?-, Verity Mackett, Ailsa Reid, Maureen Wildman, Thelma Riley, Revd K.W. Wright (Vicar of St Mary's), Harry Carpenter (Bishop of Oxford), Revd C.L.G. Hutchings (Vicar of St Giles'), Revd J.E. Taylor (Vicar of St George the Martyr, Wolverton), -?-, Anne Colborne, Judith Sawford, -?-, Margaret Crouch. Others are: Christine Batters, Jacqueline Carlile, Rosamunde Sills, Roderick Shuler (not identified).

An aerial view of St Mary the Virgin Church, vicarage and parish room. To the right is Mansfield, now Otley House, with Clarence Road in the background. St Mary's was erected in 1864 and served the area for over a hundred years before its closure after the morning service on Palm Sunday 1968. It now serves as a community centre.

St Mary's Servers, c. 1938. Back row, left to right: Bill Clark, Cecil Bailey, Claude Bailey, Les Cooper, Jack Gould, Bill Rowledge, Douglas Rose, Ted Waine, Ernie Buswell, Ted Pratt. Front row: Les Drinkwater, George Shurmer, Dennis Lovell, Revd E.J. Payne, Sam Abbot, Alan Rose.

St Mary's Mothers' Union, *c.* 1921. Back row, left to right -?-, -?-, -?-, Mrs Jane Bailey, Mrs Ada Cooper, Mrs Elizabeth Lovell, -?-, Mrs Timms, Mrs Florence Waine, Mrs Crossman. Second row: Mrs Grace, Mrs Faulkner, Mrs Rose, -?-, Mrs Forder, Mrs Lambert, -?-, Mrs Gould, Mrs Clark, -?-, Mrs Read. Third row: Mrs Robinson, Mrs Phillips, -?-, -?-, -?-, -?-, -?-, -?-, Mrs Sibthorp, -?-, Mrs Smith. Front row: Mrs Butcher, -?-, Mrs Meakins, -?-, Mrs Hugh Williams (MU leader), Revd E. Greaves (Vicar), Mrs Greaves, -?-, -?-, Mrs Joyce, Mrs Taylor, -?-. Sitting in front: Mrs Bertha Buswell with Alf, Mrs Wheeler with Ron.

The play *Maypole Morning* by Harold Brighouse being performed by St Mary's Guild Players on the Vicarage lawn in 1948. Left to right: Eric Sansom, Joan Hobson, Bill Rowledge, Betty Clarke, Barbara Knight, Connie Shean, Mrs Wood, Josie Turner, Mrs Lovell, Mary Flint, Ruth Claydon, Bill Clarke, Margaret Barden, Eileen Waine, Joy Aylott, Douglas Dillow, Ken Shean, Isabel Dillow, Betty Shurmer. The producer was Miss Zillah Full.

SECTION TWO
A Circular Tour

Just finished delivering the mail! The two postmen outside Hanslope post office in 1918 are George Valentine, wearing his war medals, and Bill Willingham jnr. There is still a post office in the village but it has moved four times within the High Street since 1918.

In the classroom of Church End School, Hanslope, 1925. The teachers are, left to right: Miss Penny, Miss Amy Tite and Miss Mathews. Pupils, left to right: Frank Atkins, Tom Clare, -?-, -?-, -?-, Betty Sutton, Ernie Garratt, Florence Ball, Dorothy Simons (front middle), Stephen Bailey, Irene Elliot, Bill Webb, -?-, -?-, -?-, Freda Clarke, Dorothy and Gladys Woodland, Dora Webb, Ted Ansell (standing), Lily Willingham, Stan Geary, Harold Powell, Walter Gable, Henry Elliott, Dorothy Stanton, Eileen Everett (side sitting), Joan Hillyer, Sid Garratt, Peggy Garratt. The classroom was lit with oil lamps, the bases of which are just visible at top of picture. Also note the coal fire, and the rubbers at the ends of the desks to clean slates.

Alexandra Rose Day was inaugurated in June 1912 to mark her fiftieth year of residence in England. Proceeds went to London hospitals. Note the Belham's bus in the background. This photograph was taken in Hanslope around 1922. The collectors include: Roda Payne, Elsie Simons, Ada Busby, Lily Yorke, Mary Gregory, Roma Eakins, Ivy Whitbread, Wyn Ditum, Nora Tebby, Hilda Kingston, Margery Haynes, Dorothy Warner, 'Sis' Gregory, Jack Eakins, Hugh Gregory, Arthur Geary.

Jack Brooks at the entrance to the old smithy which he worked for about forty years, photographed in 1968 when he was in his seventies. The spire of Hanslope Church (in the background), is perhaps the finest in the county.

Salcey Forest, Hanslope, *c.* 1910. The men are barking – stripping off oak bark to be used for tanning leather. They worked in teams of eight.

Harry Wells with the church weathervane. Hanslope's first Squire's father, William Watts, was Governor of Fort William, Bengal. When attacked by a ferocious hound, he was saved from its jaws when an arrow pierced one of its feet, and he later had both dog and arrow embodied in his coat of arms.

The Green Man Inn, The Square, Hanslope, run by publican Mrs Eakins, closed in 1956. Note the unusual chimney window. The fireplace in the room below had a chimney up to the window, which then travelled inside the roof until reaching the chimney on top of the main roof. This part of the chimney was then swept from the window!

Stan Platten's main occupation was photography. As village photographer, some of his photos are now in the Hanslope archives. Living lastly in the High Street, he died in the 1950s. This bier is now in Bucks County Museum, Aylesbury.

This postcard was sold as a souvenir of the George V Silver Jubilee celebrations, 6 May 1935. Bill Worker snr and Mr Nicholls (on the right) are outside Castlethorpe post office which is decorated for the occasion.

The villagers gathered for the unveiling of Castlethorpe War Memorial, 2 April 1921. The cottage has the date 1763 above the door and is known as the 'chocolate box cottage'. The cottage to the right was a butcher's shop, now demolished.

The 'Jolly Miller'! Andrew Nichols, photographed with his granddaughter Elizabeth, was the miller at Castlethorpe Mill from 1881 to around 1906; for some of this period he lived at Hartwell.

A successful Castlethorpe ambulance team with their first aid trophies, c. 1960s. Standing, left to right: W. Taylor, A.C. Nichols, C. Hopkins. Sitting: ? Pateman (Castlethorpe's last Stationmaster), L. Robinson, E. Green.

Castlethorpe village from the station, *c.* 1904. The station was opened in 1882 and closed on 4 September 1964. Mr Farmer Amos of Old Stratford was present at both opening and closure.

After the fire at Castlethorpe, 4 August 1905. Postcard – George, Castlethorpe to Mr. Chas. Lumb, Jnr. Westcliffe-on-Sea "Can you recognise the writer on contra side, at the fire?" A postcard from Dora to Mr Cussons, Old Trafford, relates that 'the whole place was ablaze. The people lived in the church which, luckily for them was situated on a hill, and that and the schools were all that remained.'

The building in the centre was built as the National School in 1867 by Lord Carrington, with accommodation for seventy children. It is now the Village Hall. The building on the right is the Carrington Arms, named after Earl Carrington KG, who was the principal landowner around 1911.

A sad picture! Widow Gates being evicted from her house in South Street, Castlethorpe, c. 1914, on the instructions of a local farmer. (A second picture shows all her belongings in the street.)

Too busy to write owing to "pressing engagement" which I have had on hand since being at

Was Yardley Gobion really full of pretty girls? This is an Edwardian postcard, printed in Saxony. The custom of sending postcards originated around 1894.

Two families pose for a photograph outside their homes, The Hill, Grafton Road, Yardley Gobion, *c.* 1910. Originally three cottages, it is now one property (No. 10). The building in the distance was one of Odell's slaughterhouses. Note the rough road surface.

The imposing front of Stonebank and the delightful cottages, with Miss Violet Atkins just visible in the doorway, stand in the centre of Yardley Gobion village. This postcard is postmarked 8 September 1910. The children in the centre are sitting on the stone bank. The age of the motorcycle caused this to be removed.

Jim Lambert, Yardley Gobion, c. 1920. In those days boys wore 'skirts' until they went to school at four years of age.

A wedding between two long established families in Yardley Gobion at St Leonard's Church, 25 July 1914. Back row, left to right: Percy Atkins, Annie Lambert, Harry Lambert, Violet Frances Atkins, Ike Lambert, Mrs Ike Lambert, Violet Horton (baby), Mrs Joe Horton, Joe Horton. Middle row: Will Horton, Alan Lambert, Bella Lambert, Algin Rupert Atkins (bridegroom), Hilda Louisa Lambert (bride), Miss Lambert. The girl in front of the middle row is unidentified. Front row: Henry Horton, Fred Horton, -?-, Daisy Atkins, George Horton, Rose Horton.

The corner of the village green, Yardley Gobion, *c.* 1910. The man with the yoke and buckets by the village pump and well is believed to be Mr Archie Atkins who used a lot of water in his job of roof thatching. To the left is the wagon shed in the rickyard of Elms Farm.

Thatched cottages, one of which was a general store, in Moor End Road, Yardley Gobion, *c.* 1910. Until housing development in 1947, the village consisted of little more than Moor End Road, the High Street, Chestnut Road and Grafton Road.

James Kightley, a bootmaker, and his wife, Priscilla, stand at their garden gate, *c.* 1910. His wife used to use a tinder box and dry leaves to light the kitchen fire. These cottages, opposite the post office/shop, are reputedly the first built in Yardley Gobion. The building behind the couple has now had the upper storey removed.

Enjoying a spin on his go-cart is Stan Kightley, photographed in the 1930s in the orchard behind his home at Church Bank, Yardley Gobion.

The Kightley family of Church Bank, Yardley Gobion, *c.* 1922. Back row, left to right: Ivy, Eileen, Fred, Freda. Front row: Fredk Charles Kightley, Tom, Hilda Eugene (née Gascoigne of Grafton Regis). Fredk Kightley always claimed that he was born by the roadside, which was perfectly true because his parents kept the toll-gates at the Potterspury Turn and the Dog's Mouth. Fredk, born in 1877, was apprenticed as a bricklayer; he had to start work at 6 a.m. and at the end of his 'time' was earning 7s weekly. He then went on to an hourly rate at 6½d. Having walked to Bradwell, if it was raining and he was unable to work, he could only draw 'hut money'. He was married wearing a pair of shoes that his father had made and he could remember his brother, Tom, shaving a goose at Cosgrove Feast.

Schoolchildren ready to start maypole dancing, their places marked out and numbered with whitening, in Highcroft Field, Yardley Gobion, 1906. Hesketh Road houses are now built on this site.

The May Day parade about to set out from the school, with the May Queen on the float, Yardley Gobion, 1906. In the background, left, is Potterspury Union Workhouse, erected in 1834, and later converted into housing by Mr W.W. Dickens.

A typical rural scene: Cosgrove Mill on the River Tove by the Priory. Sadly, the mill burnt down in the 1960s.

A pleasant view of Lower End, Cosgrove, below the aqueduct, c. 1900. The row of houses on the left, New Buildings, are all we can recognize today. The building on the right, formerly the Plough Inn, is now a bungalow, but the rest were swept away for redevelopment.

The church of St Peter and St Paul has stood proudly in Cosgrove since the thirteenth century. The tower was added in the fourteenth century. The lovely chestnut tree has not been there in living memory. This is now the entrance to Medlar House, formerly the Rectory.

Perhaps one of the most picturesque 'fairytale' cottages in the area is the Lodge at the entrance to Cosgrove Hall.

The ornate bridge at Cosgrove is quite the most beautiful on the whole stretch of the canal. The Grand Junction Company built it in a Gothic style, at the insistence of the then landowner. Samson's design included niches for four statues, two on each side.

The coming of the canal in 1805 bisected the village of Cosgrove but the aqueduct provided a pedestrian link. Canal horses could be brought down here to be taken to stables and blacksmiths near the Barley Mow Inn.

An early motorbike with a wickerwork sidecar, believed to have been once owned by Joseph 'Puffer' Atkinson of Cosgrove Priory. He 'puffed' with pursed lips, hence his nickname!

Joan Higgins of Elm Farm, Cosgrove, with her motorbike, custom-built by Don Freestone from oddments pre-1939, and purchased for £4 after selling two pet lambs! The front wheel was larger than the back, it had an enormous saddle which could carry a 13-stone man, a 500cc engine, and a maximum speed of only 30 mph (downhill) – but it felt like flying!

Do you like our guys? Jim Lambert and Ethel Barby with Chris Whitaker collecting rubbish for Guy Fawkes night, 1936. In the background are Church Cottages, Cosgrove, which were formerly almshouses.

Old age pensioners in Cosgrove Victory Hall, *c.* 1940s. Back row, left to right: Sam Williams, -?-, Bert Gascoigne, -?-, Bob Pettifer, Ernie Lambert, -?-. Middle row: Mr Hinton, Mrs Hinton, Mrs Valentine, Mr Valentine, Joe Castle, Mrs Castle, -?-, Mrs Bushell. Front row: Mrs Pettifer, Mrs Eglesfield snr, -?-, Frank Hillyer, Mrs Hillyer, Mercy Clark, -?-, Mrs Alderton, Mr Alderton.

Named after the tree that grew in front of them, these are Myrtle Cottages, Cosgrove. Only 20 ft away from the canal, and below the level of the water, these cottages were often flooded when the water was high. Their rear entrance steps can still be seen near the aqueduct, but the site is now an industrial development.

A bellringers' outing organized by Fred Tustain, Cosgrove, c. 1950s. Back row, left to right: Jack Chance, Frank Eydon, Vic Adams, Alec Coley, Bert Edwards. Second row: Reg Howson, Arthur Mansfield, Arthur Armstrong, Fred Case (wearing cap), John Higgins, Hedley Tustain. Third row: Bert Daniels, Tommy Roberts, Tom Trasler, Bob Abrahams, Billy Dillow. Fourth row: -?-, -?-, Mrs Bill French, Edie Daniels, Mrs Case, Doll Tustain. Front row: Bill French, Edie Sharp, Mrs Reg Howson, Mrs Dillow, Mrs Ethel Tustain, Mrs Adams. The girl (front right) is unidentified.

These keen Cosgrove players had every reason to look pleased with themselves for they had just scooped the Second Division Cup in the North Bucks and District Football League in the 1927/8 season. Back row, left to right: R. Brown (Chairman), E. Hillyer, C. Gidman, F. Johnson, G. Stewart, H. Johnson (Treasurer). Middle row: T. Cummings (Trainer), A. Noble, C. Knight (Captain), F. Barby, A. Giles, S. Bushel, W. Luck, F. Hillyer, A Meakins. Front row: Miss I. Knight (secretary), R. Giles, C. Wain, H. Cook, W. Birdsey, S. Eglesfield, Mrs Atkinson (President).

Jimmy Holman in his spinal carriage, *c.* 1930, when he lived in Old Stratford. He was for some years fishing bailiff for Cosgrove gravel pits, for which he used a motorized invalid carriage.

Women's Institute summer meeting at The Priory, Cosgrove, June 1950. Back row, left to right: Miss Gertrude Marlow, Kathleen Jones, Ethel Gallop, Dora Feil, Joan Brockway, Edith Brockway, Daisy Davis, Gertie Chown, Miss Ruby Kitson (of New Zealand), Wyn Childs, Mona Hickford, Mrs Alderton, Alice Fitzgibbon. Middle row: -?-, Linda Lyman, Daisy Gascoigne, Florrie Castle, Mercy Clarke, Mrs Bill Ratcliffe. Front row: Mrs Malcolm Jelley, Dorothy Hebson, Olive Johnson, Nellie Whitaker, Annie Tompkins.

Celebrating the Coronation of Queen Elizabeth II in Cosgrove Victory Hall, 2 June 1953. Back row, left to right: Dick Longman, Myrtle Hillyer, Rose Cummings, Ethel Barby, Harry Cummings, Fred Barby, Albert Tompkins, Don Chown. Second row: Bob Brown, Mrs Malcolm Jelley, Mrs Rickaby, Mrs Castle, Olive Eglesfield, Lil Longman, Annie Tompkins, Cynthia Tompkins, Mrs Sid Ratledge, Edie Barby, -?-, Ena Lavington, Fred Tustain, Brenda Goodridge, Sylvia Whickham, Floss Lawson, Agnes Spence, Mrs George Noble. Third row: 'Adgie' Ratcliffe, Wyn Harris, Doll Hebson, Doris Smith, Doll Tustain, Clara Williams. Fourth row: Mrs Alf Smith (standing), Alf Smith, Charlie Hill, Dora Feil, Joan Eglesfield, Carol Prater, Vince Lovesey, Dick Clark, Fred Williams, Mrs Dick Clark, Arthur Noble. Front row: Mona Hickford, Mim Eglesfield, Sue Eglesfield (baby), Gladys Loughrey, Mabel Castle, Beryl Tompkins, Audrey Smith, Ada Eglesfield, Dot Cadd, Doll Williams, Pearl Lawson, David Betts. Children: John Fitzgibbon, Roy Giles, Jimmy Pack, Tony Hefford, Billy Pack, Douglas Hillyer, Roger Kightley, Janet Eglesfield.

'It's a job like this when we sing all the songs we know and a few we don't, what a row!' Elsie, Doris and Olive, all members of the Women's Land Army hoeing turnips at Sir Hereward Wake's, Courteenhall, during the Second World War.

All clutching souvenir mugs, the children were celebrating King George V's Silver Jubilee at The Priory, Cosgrove, 6 May 1935. Front row, left to right: June Gallop, Beryl Tompkins, May Stewart, Betty Hillyer, Nancy Martin, Mabel Castle, Dennis Tompkins, Bob Gallop, Doug Hillyer, Georgie Hill.

Anyone for a Sunday afternoon ramble? Jack Johnson, a baker for 'Doughy' Norman at Cosgrove village baker, with a group of children on one of their weekly rambles, c. 1948. Back row, left to right: Pat Bushell, Dolly Williams, Sheila Brown, Rosemary Hebson, Linda Pollard, Esther Benson, Roger Kightley, Rodney Hickford, Phil Tustain, Trevor Tustain, Tony Pollard. Middle row: June Smith, Jo Hebson, -?-, Ivor Hickford, Carol Prater, Eileen Prisley, Dickie Clark, Marlene Noble, Tony Lavington, Hazel Lavington. Front row: Jill Hebson, Michael Gascoigne, -?-, Colin Bushell, -?-, Alan Tustain, Roger Pollard, Jack Johnson.

The opening of the Memorial Hall, Old Stratford, 28 May 1920. Front row, third from left: Charlie Andrews; fourth from left: Charles Sibthorp; fifth from left: Charlie Holman. Extreme right: Charlie Mundy. The hall was built to welcome home the local young men returning from the First World War and to provide a place for them to meet for social evenings. The hall cost £761 to build: some money was raised by the annual Whitsuntide 'Old English Fêtes', and the balance was given by Mr and Mrs W.W. Dickens.

First mentioned in 1734, the Falcon Inn stood at the crossroads in Old Stratford. It closed in 1924 and has been demolished. The lady is Mrs Sibthorp with her grandson, Charlie Sibthorp.

Bathing the baby 1930s style, with an old zinc bath in front of the fire. An unknown family from Old Stratford.

Ellen Holman making pillowlace at her home, 9 Cosgrove Road, Old Stratford. Formerly a Miss Taylor of Calverton, her husband, Harry Holman, had been licensee of the Shoulder of Mutton, Calverton, around 1900.

Ron Hall of Old Stratford sporting the very latest fashion in the 1930s – a hand-knitted jumper suit.

Mothers Union ladies enjoying a pleasant summer afternoon at Passenham Manor, 1906.

St Guthlac's Church, Passenham. Its main structure was erected in the thirteenth century. It has a ring of five bells, the treble being medieval. There are eighteenth-century box pews. The chancel is noted for its murals, while the parish charities are painted on the gallery.

Interior, Passenham Church. The Jacobean carved oak pulpit, with its lofty sounding board, features four emblems representing the kingdoms incorporated in the Stuart arms: the rose and crown for England, the thistle for Scotland, the fleur-de-lis for France and the harp for Ireland. It was installed around 1800.

The water mill, Passenham, was built in the mid-seventeenth century and ceased operating around 1920. The River Ouse, which flows right under the mill, can be viewed through a glass-bottomed floor in one of the rooms. Photograph by Sylvia Clarke, *c.* 1938.

After the fire at E. & H. Roberts Ltd, Millwrights, Brass and Iron Founders, Deanshanger, on 11 September 1912. Harry Cooper records on this postcard: 'Wolverton Fire Brigade 14 minutes; Stony Stratford F.B. 7 mins; Walter and I cycled 5 mins.' The business closed in 1929.

A winning team – Deanshanger Football Club. Back row, left to right: Perce Jones, Verdun Parker, Ernie Long, Dill Jones, Jack Burton, Bill Coxhill, Ben Bull, Les Roberts, Alan Blair, Doug Foddy, Darrell Case. Front row: Alma ('Taffy') Maycock, Jack Willett, Cyril Ridgeway, Dennis Church, Cyril Nicholls. The club had a very successful period in the late 1940s and early 1950s in the North Bucks League, and in 1947 they won the Towcester Hospital Cup. They reached the finals again in 1948 but this time they lost. Their success came under the very keen secretaryship of Douglas Foddy and a strong committee.

The corner of High Street and Boswell Lane, Deanshanger, *c.* 1950s. The shop was formerly John Eales' general stores and was later run by his son Laurie, a well-known organist, as a clothes shop. Later it was Billy Boots' gents' hairdressing and general stores. Notice the advertisements: R. White's ginger ale and seltzer; Glosso; Sunlight soap and Ingersoll watches. The shop is now a private house.

Frank Davis, Eve Neal and Isabell Davis by the wall in Little London, Deanshanger, *c.* 1930. The old Rose and Crown Inn is visible in the distance. This view is completely obscured today by trees and development.

The Deanshanger Friendship Club, formed in 1956, enjoying their annual tea at Passenham Manor, *c.* 1958. Back row, left to right (standing): Mrs Evans, Mrs A. Reynolds, Mrs M. Henson, Mrs W. Pope, Mrs McNeil, Mrs B. Moore, Mrs R. Roberts, Mrs L. Tompkins, Mrs G. Dumbleton, Mrs J. Whittemore, Mrs J. Brewer, Mrs J. Smith, Mrs S. Masters, Nurse Webb, Mrs P. Baker, Lady Roberts, The Hon. Mrs Flora Lawson. Sitting at tables, nearest camera, left to right: -?-, -?-, -?-, -?-, -?-, -?-, Mrs W. Reynolds, Mr G. Barby, Mrs G. Barby, Mr W. Green, Mrs W. Green, Mrs Foddy, Mrs Dave Tapp, Mr Joe Tapp, Mr Dave Tapp.

Hidden behind the thatched cottage known as 'The Lighthouse' (demolished before 1939) is the Smithy, Deanshanger, owned by Luke Roberts, whose business was carried on by his eldest son, Eden John. The Brook is in the foreground, and the houses on the left are in Patrick's Lane.

Interior of the Smithy, Deanshanger. On the right is Eden Roberts, on the left is Arthur Roberts (son). The man in the centre is unknown. The Smithy closed on the death of Arthur Roberts.

Formed by the Revd Paul Hoskin in the early 1930s the Boy Scouts troop here give a cycle display at Deanshanger fête, 4 September 1938, on Mr Montgomery's lawn at Manor Farm, The Green. The left-hand group is: Francis Nicholls, Bob Canvin, Gordon Roberts (on bicycles), Arch Roberts, Beryl Church (on top). The right-hand group is: Ben Bull, William Henson, Bunt Longland (on bicycles), Ron Goldney, Derek Smith (on top). The only troop in Northamptonshire to give tumbling and cycle displays, they were trained by an army friend of Revd Hoskin. They went as far afield as Wellingborough and Kettering as well as to Whittlebury, Paulerspury, Stony Stratford and Wicken Park. Their speciality was an evening display to music, where Lampitt & Elliott of Wolverton provided the tannoy, and a lighting system on the two groups where blue and yellow changed to green and red. The troop consisted mostly of Deanshanger boys, with the Scout headquarters at Wicken Rectory, where four patrols each had a room. Lady Penrhyn wished to be associated with the troop and special permission was obtained from Scout headquarters for the troop to bear the title 'Lady Penrhyn's Own'. The County of Northamptonshire, where the troop was registered, was the only one to have its name on the front of the Scout hat leather band. They won the Northants County Sports Competition and also the County Nature Shield at Corby and Courteenhall. Several boys went to the World Jamboree at Moisson, France with Revd Hoskin. At the commencement of the Second World War, Revd Hoskin went to serve his country in the Royal Navy and the troop was disbanded, and sadly never reformed.

May Day, Deanshanger, *c.* 1933. Back row, left to right: Joan Grant, Leslie Drinkwater, Dorothy Holman, William Henson, Beryl Church, Elsie Nicholls, Graham Cooper, Hilda Cooper, Gordon Roberts, Gladys Price. Front row: Linda Hall, Peter Wyatt, Phyllis Harris (May Queen), Ken Reynolds, Gladys Pratt.

Reg Tite, fishing at Deanshanger, *c.* 1926/7. A budding fisherman, he was perhaps reflecting on that big one that got away!

Deanshanger Primary School, *c.* 1958. Back row, left to right: Alan Holloway, Colin Read, Bobby Hollis, Robert Marshall, Leslie Drinkwater, Graham Hamilton, John Frost, Mrs Walton (teacher). Middle row: ? Drinkwater, Martin Smith, Jennifer Hamilton, Jackie Fielding, -?-, Kathleen Peach, Sonia Lea, -?-. Front row: Julie Golding, Rosemary Church, Christine Blackwell, Christine Gedge, -?-, Linda Tolley, Elaine Clark, Susan Ridgeway Margaret Henson, Pat Francis, Tricia Andrews. Sitting on ground: Roger Andrews, Kevin O'Brien.

Children in fancy dress for the Coronation of Queen Elizabeth II festivities, 2 June 1953, outside Deanshanger Memorial Hall, known as 'the tin hut'. Some of those in the front row are: Ernest Kauffman, Barbara Church, Roger Andrews, Peter Roberts, Carol Ridgeway, Alan Russell, Colin Read, Michael Read, Christine Bull, Jillian Henson, Margaret Henson, Lawrence King, Jonathan Nicholls, Geoffrey Church, ? Pratt. Mrs Watson, the schoolteacher, is second from the right at the back. Sid Bird and Jim Roberts are on the right. Each child in fancy dress received a Coronation pencil.

Deanshanger Girls' Life Brigade in the early 1960s. Front row, right to left: Lynne Ayris (escort), -?- (flagbearer), Valerie Higgs (escort). Behind them are Miss Phyllis Picketts (Captain), -?-, Pat Alderman, Margaret Henson, -?-, Julie Golding and ? Andrews.

'What do you think of these little girls just out of school?', writes the sender of this postcard, dated 1907. They are outside Wicken School with Mr 'Curly' Green the headmaster.

Pushing the perambulator in Crosstree Road, Wicken, is Edith Clara Giles with her great-nephew, George John Whitehead, and under the pram hood, Margaret Whitehead, her great-niece. The photograph was taken around 1905.

A row of houses near the White Lion public house (now the Wicken Arms). Note the little thatched cottage in background – one could touch the eaves when walking beneath them, it was so low. Sadly it has been demolished.

The fair at Wicken, *c.* 1906. The smallest boy standing in the centre in front of Sheppard's Roundabouts is George John Whitehead.

Whitsuntide, Wicken, 1907. On the right is Mrs Mary Jane Whitehead, with her two children, George John and Margaret.

Wicken Hospital Fête, 1920s. Every village held an annual fête to raise money for Northampton General Hospital. The photograph was taken on the Rectory's front drive and includes Edith Mary Giles (Red Cross), third from left on cart; Gladys Eden (Red Cross), sitting third from left; Violet Birdsey, sitting fourth from left; Maggie Birdsey, sitting sixth from left.

Bert Wrighton cooking Christmas turkeys at the Bakehouse, Wicken, *c.* 1949. Sunday dinners were baked for the villagers, commencing at 11 a.m., also 'cakes, tarts and taters'. His father, Freddie Walton, champion hedge-layer, owned a part of Wicken Wood from which Bert collected faggots to light the oven.

Wicken Church bells and bellringers, 22 March 1931. From left to right: Walt Jackson, George ('Jack') Foddy, Tom Read, George Cooper, G.J. Whitehead, Harry Cashmore, Len Smith, Fred Walton, Cyril Warner, Tommy Roberts, Harry Ridgeway, Freddie Pateman, Freddie Case, Jack Green jnr, Jack Green snr, George Green snr, Hubert Brown, William Buckingham, Canon W. Alex Carroll, Edgar Shakeshaft, Fred Cashmore and the rector's dog.

A country scene at Upper Weald, Calverton, c. 1900. The Woodbine public house, now demolished, was in the paddock to the right. Templars is no longer thatched.

Little changed through the centuries: the seventeenth-century Manor Farm Cottages, Lower Weald, Calverton, *c*. 1930. Left to right: Mrs Godfrey (in doorway), little Alfie Bull (a hunchback), Mr Godfrey, -?-, -?-. Girls in front: Eunice Petty, Edie Miller.

Another view of Lower Weald, Calverton. The spring has been diverted under the road from the Rectory Farm entrance, and the cottages are no longer thatched, but the railings (left) are still *in situ*.

A 14 ft steel 'Hercules' wind engine,
manufactured by E. & H. Roberts Ltd,
Deanshanger Ironworks, erected at
Manor Farm, Calverton, *c.* 1902.
Photograph by Mitch Hicks.

Near the Cross Hills Bridge on the
road leading to Calverton, 'Gorrick's
Spring' waters gush from the lion's
mouth. In years gone by the monks of
Stony Stratford, who lived where The
Retreat now stands, deemed this
wayside spring to be sacred, possessed
of healing properties, and they used the
waters to cure their ailing flock.

Now nestling behind trees, the ancient church of the Assumption of St Mary the Virgin at Beachampton, dates from the fourteenth century and has a wooden shingled spire. It contains a seventeenth-century marble monument to Simon Bennet Esq., Lord Mayor of London, who was the nephew of Sir Simon Bennet, once lord of the manor.

This peaceful scene in Watery Lane, Beachampton, is no longer recognizable, although the area retains its rural atmosphere. Red House Farm is unchanged but Ivy Cottage has long since disappeared, replaced by Brookside and Homestall.

Mary Ann Smith (Polly), born 1869, the proud owner of the first ladies' cycle in Beachampton, *c*. 1889.

The Bell Inn, Beachampton, still retains its village setting but is no longer thatched and has been extensively altered.

Beachampton cricket team, *c.* 1910. Back row, left to right: F. Lovell, R. Linney, J. Weatherhead, B. Warren, Mr Slater, E. Lovell, P. Edwards. Middle row: J. Godfrey, F. Whiting. Front row: C. Bailey, A. Gibbs, G. Franklin, S. Bailey.

Beachampton School, *c.* 1895. The teachers are Miss Hall and Miss Whithead but the pupils' names are not known. The school was built in 1869 for forty children.

Tedding hay by hand, Grange Farm, Beachampton, 1919. Left to right: Christopher Lovell, -?-, George Franklin, Bert Warren, Martin Farmer.

A common sight in the past: rows of stooks of corn drying in the field before being carted. Each stook consisted of ten to twelve bound sheaves leaning against one another in two rows; the rows were aligned north/south so that each side got the maximum warmth from the sun. Photograph by J. Starsmore.

A tranquil scene by Nash pond: Edie Smith with her yoke and buckets while her husband, Rube Smith, is resting on his barrow from his work as roadman. On the far side a cow quenches its thirst.

Wood End, Nash. A boy stands by the bicycle of W.J. Rhodes, photographer, of Mursley. The small building in front of the cottage was a pig sty.

Nash Band outside the New Inn, *c.* 1910. Standing (left side): George Weatherhead; right side: Jack Saunders. Back row, left to right: Ernest and Arthur Smith, Jim Weatherhead (drummer), Bill Neal, Bill Mackerness. Front row: Amos Weatherhead, Aiden Smith, Harry Illing, George Colton, Ernest Pitkin, Mark Smith.

The wood yard and sawmill, Nash, *c.* 1930. Brothers Lawrence and Wilfred Varney are hand sawing. This timber business was started by their father Mr George Varney.

Nash School, *c.* 1916. Pupils, back row, left to right: -?-, Madge Colton, Kate Smith, Henry Weatherhead, Nelly Jones, Bill Smith, George Watts, Ena Knight. Middle row: Win Smith, Laurence Varney, Emily Dunkley, Billy Knight. Front row: May Varney, Albert Smith, Eric Saunders, Ethel and Kathleen French (twins), Eric Hatherington, Bella and Alice Armitage (twins), Ambrose Weatherhead.

Henry Weatherhead with Harwood's bread cart, Nash, *c.* 1919. Standing in the doorway is probably Florrie Cooney.

The final parade of Nash Home Guard, 3 December 1944. Back row, left to right: Reg Watts, Bill Weatherhead, Jack Wall, Lawrence Varney, Alf Stanton, Bill Threader, Eric Mackerness, Aubrey Varney, Ken Orchard, Tom Orchard, Fred King. Front row: Bill Bailey, Arthur Wyatt, Fred Cowley, Wilfred Varney, Fred Wall, Arthur Smith, Fred Linney.

The Old Bakehouse, No. 9 Stratford Road, Nash, c. 1907. Fred and Clara Harwood pose with their children Mercy and Selby. The notice over the bakehouse reads F.S. Harwood, Baker & Mealman.

Pink's End and Church Lane from Whaddon Church tower. The former takes its name from Parson Pink who lived in the Vicarage here (now Whaddon House).

Harry Cowley with his bicycle near the Lowndes Arms, Whaddon, *c.* 1930. Harry kept a shop in Vicarage Road and also had a milk round. He later moved to Bletchley where he started a garage. The Vicarage Road shop was taken over by Mrs Jinks but is now closed.

Mrs King out for a drive in her 'Sunday best', with St Mary's Church, Whaddon, on the promontory in the background.

The last robed Whaddon Church choir. Back row, left to right: Hugh Willett, Revd Dilworth, Jack Nicholson. Boys: Peter Nicholson, Alan Justice, Patrick Nicholson, Robert Justice, Bernard Howell.

A concert party at Whaddon, *c.* 1937. 'When grandpapa asked grandmama for the second minuet' was produced by Mr Tesh in the village hall. Centre: Mr Tesh, Mrs King. The cast includes: Fred Hayward, Ron Missenden, Jess Higgs, Hugh Willett, Lilian Adams, Evelyn Reynolds. Note the Pierrot costumes: men wore black with gold sash and pom poms, women wore gold with black accessories.

Bert, Ada and George Willett, a lovely Whaddon family group, *c.* 1906. The boys are wearing lace collars, probably hand-made by their grandmother, Betsy Willett of Shenley.

The Hayward family lived in this wattle and daub house on Common, now Vicarage Road. It was demolished in 1960. The girl in the doorway is Ena Knight.

Whaddon British Legion, Women's Section, *c.* 1950s. Their banner was dedicated at Whaddon Church by the Bishop of Buckingham. At the front of the parade are Colonel Strettell and Mr Weatherby. Next row: Evelyn Jaworski (standard-bearer), Margaret Illing and Connie Bowden (escorts). In the Men's Section: Ted Roff (flagbearer), Mr Bill Hopkins and Mr Harry Varney (escorts). Founder of the Whaddon Branch was Mrs De Silva of Little Horwood (at the back, wearing a large hat).

Whaddon Guides and Brownies, c. 1930s. Back row, left to right: Freda Shakeshaft, Edna Powell, Eva Peverill, Ruby Facey, Mabel Nicholson. Middle row: Daisy Peverill, -?-, Sylvia King, Miss Moore (Captain), Kath Taylor, Hazel Robinson. Front row: Marjorie Wood, Hilda Barnes, Lilian Adams, Rita Shakeshaft, Flossie Peverill.

Whaddon School, *c.* 1917/18. Back row, left to right: Fred Hayward, Beat Keyes, Irene Hobbs, -?-, Florrie Taylor, Mabel Summers, Enid Greenaway, Doris Wrighton. Second row: Gwen Lovell (teacher), ? Hobbs, Ted Hayward, George Young, Hugh Willett, George Faulkner, Edgar Faulkner, George James, Ted Wrighton, Miss Curran (Headmistress). Third row (sitting): Annie Tofield, Ada Willett, Gwen Harley, Kath Taylor, Winifred James, Queenie Young, ? Hobbs. Front row: Eva Willett, Amy Willett, Reg Faulkner, Annie Illing.

Whadden School cricket team, *c.* 1915. Back row, left to right: ? Curtis, -?-, Bill Taylor, -?-, Seymour ('Jack') Higgs. Front row: Bert Willett, -?-, Billy Goodway (with bat), Fred Keyes, George Willett, -?-.

Ted Hayward of Whaddon, Champion Blackberry Picker of North Bucks, photographed *c.* 1917. The blackberries were sold to raise money for the war effort.

Whaddon School football team, 1923. Back row, left to right: Hugh Willett, Ted Hayward, Edmund Bryant, George James. Middle row: Charlie Justice, -?-, Eric Hall, Bill French. Front row: -?-, Ted Wrighton (with football), Reg Faulkner.

Mrs King feeding a ewe and her quads at Pear Tree Farm, Whaddon, *c.* 1930s. This ewe brought up quad lambs for four consecutive years.

Mr Dorian Williams, last Master of the Whaddon Chase, heads the cavalcade of riders, *c.* 1950s. William (Bill) Kingston, on the bicycle, was a member of one of the first Hunt Supporters' Clubs, the Whaddon Chasers, which was formed in 1955. The hunt amalgamated with the Bicester and Warden Hill Hunt during the 1986–7 season to become the Bicester with Whaddon Chase Hunt.

Teddy Masters, head groom for Mr Selby-Lowndes at Shenley Park, lived at Stag Lodge, Shenley. He is seen here as the amateur huntsman who blew the horn for Whaddon Chase Hunt.

Carol singing at Howe Park Farm, Tattenhoe, *c.* 1960s. Back row, left to right: Hugh Willett, Alice Justice, Evelyn Jaworski, Revd Dilworth, -?-, -?-. Front row: Hilary Cross, ? Howell, Patrick Nicholson, Richard Formella, Mrs Strettell, wife of Colonel E.F.D. Strettell, Peter Nicholson. Bernard Howell. Whaddon Church choir visited all the outlying farms as well as Whaddon village.

Bellringers of Shenley, left to right: George Clarke, Ernest ('Shoppy') Willett, Frank Robinson, Will Daniels, Revd Joe Vincent, Sid Willett (verger), Cecil Burgess, Hugh Cameron. The bells were recast in 1908.

This fête was held to raise money to build a hall for Shenley Brook End. Back row, left to right: Albert Rodway, Bill Rodway, -?-, -?-, Doug Grace, Herbert Capel, Albert Shouler, Charles Hooton (holding umbrella), George Masters, Fred Rodway, Teddy Masters. Front row: Harry Coleman, Ken Willett, Arthur Daniels, Reg Willett (on cart), Ern Willett, Sid Willett, Fred Kimble.

This steam engine, built by W. Allchin, brass founders at Global Works, St James End, Northampton, was owned by John Hooton. it powered the threshing box but could not move under its own steam and had to be pulled by horses. It remained in use until the 1980s when it was destroyed. Threshing at Rectory Farm, Shenley Brook End, in September 1910, are (left to right): Thomas Walduck, Arthur Irons Willett, Cecil Willett, George Capel, Herbert Robinson, George Eaton, Alfred Harris, John Hooton, Alfred Daniels, Joseph Willett, George Payne.

The opening of Shenley Brook End Village Hall, 10 May 1930. Back row, left to right:
Harold Daniels, Mrs Jack Markham, Jack Markham, Mr Grange, Albert Rodway, Sid
Daniels, Mabel Willett, Sid Willett. Second row: Mrs Perry, Mrs Polly Ward, Harry
Hands, Herbert Capel, Arthur Daniels, Bill Rodway, Mrs Albert Bass, Charlie Roberts,
Mrs Charlie Roberts, Charlie Hooton, Mrs Charlie Hooton, Mr Clark, Mrs Clark, Ted
Shouler, Mr Powell (holding Robert Powell). Third row (sitting): Mrs Mona Ball, Rose
Daniels, Mrs Fred Rodway, Mrs Grange, Mrs Weatherley, Ern Willett, Frank Hodson,
Fred Rodway, Mrs Herbert Capel, Mrs George Grace, Mrs Freddie Cox, Mrs Ern
Willett, Mrs Emma Daniels. Front row: Bert Bowler, Ted Ward, Bert Shouler, Trixie
Hobbs, Freda Rodway, Constance Rodway, Fred Kimble. Stan Ball, Albert Bass. Charlie
Roberts, the oldest person, planted a tree at the opening ceremony.

Rose and Crown, Shenley Brook End, is now a private house, Green View. Mrs Mona Ball still resides here. Nellie, the writer of the postcard, says, 'This is the latest taken of the house, 1907'.

Shenley Brook End.

Shenley Brook, c. 1930s. Surely there is nothing to equal this lovely view.

A cottage industry of yesteryear: making pillowlace, *c.* 1903. Left to right: Mrs Fanny Fleet, Mrs Capel, Priscilla Daniels (later Mrs Cox), Mrs Betsy Willett, Mrs Jenkins (wearing lace cap). Mrs Jenkins lived on a nearby farm; the others all lived in Primrose Square. Priscilla Daniels was the village schoolteacher at Shenley Church End for more than fifty years.

Florrie Cooper in Primrose Square, Shenley Brook End (now demolished). The X marks the cottage where her grandmother, Betsy Willett, lived and outside which the lacemakers are working in the photograph above.

Shenley Cricket Team, winners of the Sympson and District Cricket League, 1922, outside the Talbot Inn, Loughton. Back row, left to right: Mr Gardener (Umpire), Albert Jones, Bill Shouler, Mr Baker, Bill Johnson, Percy Goodway, Mr Alderman of Old Bradwell (Umpire). Front row: Fred Jones, Edwin Higgs, Walt Elliott (Captain), Tom Gregory, Ern Johnson. Sitting on ground: Arthur Lane, Alastair Cameron.

The pedigree Dairy Shorthorn herd was built up by Jesse Ebbs at Manor Farm, Shenley Church End from around 1919. His son, Frank, is seen here with the Shorthorn cows that won the top (100 guineas) prize at Reading Show, 1942/3. Frank competed with his Shorthorns at shows all over the country from 1930 until 1971, when the herd was sold.

Haymaking at Manor Farm, Shenley Church End, in the 1920s. Ricks like this continued to be made until the advent of the baler in the early 1950s.

Shenley School, *c.* 1921. Back row, left to right: Lena Higgs, Elsie Jackman, Evelyn Gregory, Edie Higgs, Marion Cox, Amy Claridge. Middle row: Teddy Higgs, Lucy Read, Fred Shouler, Phyllis Willett, Nell Ward, Irene Gregory, Bert Daniels, Dorothy Wyatt, -?-, ? Jackman. Front row (standing): Bill Higgs, Phyllis Claridge, Ruth Higgs; sitting: Ida Higgs, Jack Dolling, Howard Dolling (with board), Emily Higgs, Bertram Wyatt, -?-.

Scouts and Guides in costume for their operetta *Princess Chrysanthemum* in 1953, produced by their Scoutmaster Revd F. Crosby of Loughton. Back row, left to right: Bill Higgs, Lesley Wick, Alan Weatherley. Middle row: Dorothy Gurney, Mac Foxley, Majorie Daniels. Front: John Willett.

A New Year's Day party in Shenley Reading Room, 1955. Clockwise from front left: Jennifer Sykes, Judith Ebbs, Ann Carter, Freda Bazeley, Doreen Masters, Dorothy Ebbs, Carolyn Ebbs (baby), Rita Sykes, Shirley Berry, Roy Goodway, Daphne Goodway, Mrs McGill, two McGill children, Hazel Weston, Miriam Bazeley, Catherine Ebbs.

Some bride! A mock wedding at Loughton, *c.* 1950s. Back row, left to right: Frank Alderman, Ted Gurney, Valerie Willett, Mrs Weatherley, Mrs Ethel Gurney, Jean Ebbs, Reg Cox, Dorothy Wells. Front row: Ken Ebbs (bridegroom), Trevor (Anon?), Penelope Dolling, Arthur Wells.

A long-established farming family, the Gurneys of Rectory Farm, Loughton, *c.* 1898. Left to right: Matthew Willett ('Uncle Matt'), Ethel Gurney, Jesse Gurney, Ted Gurney, Minnie Gurney (née Dickens), Margaret Gurney.

William Willett and his wife, Mary Ann Cox of Shenley, emigrated to Australia in 1857. They sailed on the *John and Lucy*, and their daughter was born at sea during the crossing. They named her Lucy Atlantic. William worked in Sydney then moved to Castlereigh and farmed. He operated a team, carting goods over the Blue Mountains to Mudgee until the railway extended over. They have many descendants in Australia.

The old shop on The Green, Loughton, was founded by Mrs J.E. Wells in 1831. Three sons, Herbert, James and Arthur, went into the business with their mother. Left to right: -?-, -?-, Lizzie Wells, Jane Esther Wells, Nellie Wells, Herbert Wells, James Wells. After the house was built, they moved to their present location in Bradwell Road. J.E. Wells & Sons, Outfitter, Footwear, Linens, is now managed by her grandson, Mr K.S. Trevor Wells.

Workers travelling by horse and wagonette to Wolverton Railway Works, *c*. 1900. The driver is probably Tommy Franklin, the farmer from Old Farm, Loughton, which is now part of Milton Keynes.

Loughton Board School, Group I, *c.* 1904/5. Back row, second from left: Arthur Wells; sixth: Ted Gurney. Third row, fourth from left: Ethel Gurney. The teacher was Mrs Buttons.

Women's Institute Senior Friends Tea at Loughton in the 1950s. Helpers, standing by wall: -?-, Olive Foxley, Mrs Kitchener, Mrs E.J. Willett, Mrs Pateman, -?-, Gwen Carter, Rose Daniels, Peggy Bodley, Marjorie Harris, Joan Harris, Mrs Hands, Mrs Spen Johnson; bottom right: Reuben Hall. Left of table: Mrs Walton, Reg Cooper, -?-, Mrs Missenden, Walt Missenden, Mr Crisp, Mrs Crisp, Percy Foxley, Ethel Foxley. Right of table: Polly Ward, Ted Ward, -?-, Mrs Collyer, -?-, Miss Burke, Mrs Higgs, Mr Higgs, Harry Willett, Mrs H. Willett, Phoebe Wells.

The Shenley and Loughton football team photographed at Sherington in the late 1940s. Back row, left to right: Harry Quinn (trainer), Maurice Goodway, Tom Markham, Maurice Daniels, Robert Willett, Aubrey Perry. Middle row: Jack Houghton, Bernard Groom, Lawrence Smith. Front row: Len Willett, Peter Hill, Les Parker, Albert Bass, Ron Daniels.

Judy the donkey takes Hannah Bird and her cousin Richard Pattenden for a ride at Payne's Farm, Loughton, c. 1918. Hannah's father, Richard Bird, built Memorial Cottages, Jubilee Cottages and five other cottages on The Green, Loughton.

Newport Nobby in full steam on the western side of Bradwell station; to the right is the Bradwell siding. The Newport Pagnell branch railway opened in 1865 and served the area for almost a hundred years. The windmill has been a feature of Bradwell since around 1817, and for a period from 1857 it was owned by Robert Adams of Bradwell Abbey.

Typical of the cottages built in New Bradwell by the railway company, Bridge Street was demolished pre-1970s.

New Bradwell Girls' School, Standard II, in the 1930s. Top row, left to right: V. Henson, H. Cowley, V. Johnson, I. Shering, P. Sprittles, B. Guntrip, P. Odell, -?-, E. Labrum, -?-. Second row: D. Holland, I. Pollard, B. Robinson, E. Tattem, L. Galtress, N. Owens, J. Varney, E. Legg, J. West, -?-. Third row: M. Kelly, I. Verrall, A. Woodward, B. Palmer, P. Shrimpton, -?-. Front row: B. Dutton, B. Sapwell, J. Tuckey, B. McLeod.

Class IIB in their classroom at Bradwell School, *c.* 1920. Note the fashions: girls wore pinafore dresses, with their hair in ringlets; boys wore sailor suits with lace collars.

Pupils of Bounty Street Boys' School, New Bradwell, *c.* 1916. Mr C. Markham, who came from Stony Stratford, was a teacher at the school for many years.

Class Junior III at Bradwell School, *c.* 1916. Mr Fred Rudman was the class teacher. Centre front is Jack Cook. Also in the photograph are: Kenneth Bird, Sydney Blackburn, Harry Brooks, Norman Bunce, Tommy Chaytor, Dennis Cook, Les Cosby, Eddie Dillow, Douglas Garner, Fred Godfrey, Alfred Goodger, Harold Grace, Eric Johnson, George Jones, Eric Lane, Alan Larkinson, Ronald Preston, Cyril Robinson, Harold Sapwell, Jim Twigg, Charles Walker, Harold Watson, Jack Williams, George Wood.

Stantonbury St Peter's AFC, season 1926/7. This team won the Stantonbury Hospital Cup, were finalists in the Bucks Junior Charity Cup, and runners up in the Bedford and District League. Back row, left to right: J. Penman, P. Lines, S. Shelton, C. Wood, A. Swain, R. Pollard. Middle row: C. Scott, H. Dowdy (Assistant Trainer), F. Strong (Captain), A. Tompkins, P. Pell, T. Ireson, V. West. Front row: W. Boddy, O. Mills (Chairman), A. Stones, A. Watson, B. Nash, W. Alderman, J. Neale, R. Mills (Honorary Secretary).

Bradwell Band at Wicken Club Day, *c.* 1936. The band was formed in 1838. Back row, left to right: Bill Matthews, Ron Smart, ? Campbell, Les Cosby, -?-, Harold Walters, Walt Kightley. Middle row: Jack Quinn, Bill Walker, Bert Breedon, -?-, Bill Walters, -?- (half-hidden). Front row: John Levitt, Les Smart, Tom Kelly, Jim Levitt.

Stantonbury Working Men's Social Club quoits team, *c.* 1920. Extreme left front, Steward Nash. These were the champions. All Working Men's Clubs had quoits beds (clay beds) at this time and the game was as popular then as darts is today. This club celebrated its centenary in March 1994.

Haversham School, November 1914. The teacher on the left is Miss Dorothy Taylor. On the extreme right is Mrs Barnardi, the Headmistress.

These premises opposite the main gates of the Railway Works encompassed three shops, photographed here around 1895. The business was founded by Samuel Coop who is standing on the left (with beard). The lad in the centre is his son William S. Coop who continued to run the business when his father retired. In the bedroom window is his daughter, Sarah Coop and on the extreme right, Michael Westgate, an apprentice who later moved to Woking, Surrey, where he became mayor. The range of goods they sold are displayed outside and advertised above the shop. They also had a horse and cart with a large drum containing paraffin which travelled around the villages. Samuel lived at the White House, Wolverton Road, Stony Stratford, and was the first person to start a hire purchase scheme in the area. He had a corrugated tin hut in North Street, New Bradwell, where his customers took their money every Saturday. They paid 6d per week in 1888.

McCorquodale & Co. Ltd opened their printing and stationery works in Wolverton in 1878. The stamping press (purchased in 1882) was used to emboss the postage stamps on registered envelopes. The man on the left (seated) is an Inland Revenue official from Somerset House.

McCorquodale & Co. Ltd billiards team, winners of the Gobey League Cup, 1929. Left to right: Fred Kaye, Bill Rowledge (Captain), Mr Herbert E. Meacham (Manager), Cyril Smith. The League was started by Mr Gobey, the Superintendent at the Railway Works, and teams included Wolverton Fire Brigade, the Railway Veterans Institute, and the Congregational and Wesleyan Chapels. The cup is now in the Railway Works archive stores.

Flat caps seemed to be the order of the day for the Joiners, Pattern Makers and Wheelwrights of the London & North Western Railway Company, Wolverton, in 1914. Back row, left to right: Jimmy Robinson, George Shean, ? Jones, 'Dummy' Bettle (who was deaf and dumb), ? Richardson, boy apprentice, Bill Roberts (later Foreman of the Moulding Shop), boy apprentice, boy apprentice, Sid Illing, ? Crisp, boy apprentice, Clarence Little, Bert Swannell, -?-. Second row: Arthur Welton, Bert Tyrrell, Bert Waine (later Foreman of the Joiners Shop 1927–51), ? Cole, ? Neal, ? Huckle, -?-, -?-, boy apprentice, Bill Munday, ? Webb, ? Old, -?-, ? Rogers. Third row: 'Fishy' Eales (shop clerk), George Snowdon jnr, ? West, Walter Parker, Jimmy Whitmee, Owen Knight, -?-, Jimmy Jones (later Foreman of the Sawmill), Percy Tew, ? Tucker, Stephen Faulkner, George Clark, S. Jones (Foreman). Front row: boy apprentice, Jack Toogood, Bob Line, -?- (bandmaster at Wolverton), 'Ratty' Herbert, ? Taylor, Harry Russell, George Snowdon snr, Jimmy Jordon, -?-, Bill Teagle, Fred Clarridge. In front: two boy apprentices.

Wages Office girls at Wolverton Railway Works, Christmas, *c.* 1950. Standing, left to right: Pat Judge, Barbara Hughes, Mary Saggers, Jill Nicholls, Kay Williams, Sheila Williams, Janet Fensom. Sitting: Marie Knowlson, Jill Merritt, Winnie Cashmore (supervisor), Betty Higby.

LMS Horticultural Society present their annual Wolverton Works Flower Show in the Mess Room, *c.* 1950s. Some of those admiring the blooms are: Patsy Gerrard, Archie Bates, Bill Tapp from Potterspury and his wife, Archie Lathall, Dorothy and Frank Stevens, Albert Townsend, Stan Baldwin, Charlie Letts.

LMS 'Fur and Feather Society', *c.* 1940s. Back row, left to right: George Stevens, Newman Willis, Jim Claydon, Solomon Gascoigne, ? Humphries, -?-, -?-, -?-. Middle row: Albert Ratley, -?-, Stan Holbrook, Cecil Atkinson, -?-, -?-, Albert Mead, Charles Crick, Cecil Valentine, Jack Alderman, Colin Smith. Front row: George Pratt, Charlie Sibthorp, Bert Craddock, Bert Walker, Frank Mayo, Bob Cockerill. Their shows were held in the Old Market Hall, Wolverton.

The LMS Cricket Team of the Wolverton Town Cricket and Associated Sports Club, were the proud winners of the LMS Cricket Challenge Cup in 1927. Back row, left to right: E.G.H. Gray (Secretary), T.T. Brinnand (Umpire), W.R. Munday, L.N. Smith, A.J. Rogoff, H.T. Curtis, A. Fields (Scorer). Middle row: F.H. Brown, F. Yates, D.L.L. Mackey (Captain), E.T. Brocklehurst (Vice-Captain), W.W. Wootton, H.J. Hollands. Front row: E. McKaig, D.R. Wills. The team representing the Wolverton Works were all railway employees there and played regularly in their own town or village clubs in the neighbouring area. They appeared in the LMS Cricket Club final in 1927, 1928 and 1929 and were winners in 1927 and 1928. This was a great achievement when one considers the competition involved all the depots on the London, Midland & Scottish Railway.

This single-cylinder Oldsmobile in 1903 is believed to have been the first motor owned by a Wolverton resident. It had a 5 hp single cylinder water-cooled engine, and a top speed of 20 mph with two gears. Mr Joseph Rainbow, a bookmaker, driving his daughter, Sarah Anne, outside the Locomotive Inn, (now the Galleon Inn).

Wolverton Fire Brigade wearing their brass helmets, c. 1920s. This is the first 'Steamer', purchased by public subscription in 1913. Photograph by Harry Cooper.

Marching band on manoeuvres at Stacey Hill Farm, Wolverton, 1913. The farm buildings in the background are now the Milton Keynes Museum of Industry and Rural Life.

The generosity of Mr A.R. Trevithick enabled the Cenotaph – a replica of those put up in London and the provinces – to be erected in Wolverton until its place could be taken by a permanent monument. The Cenotaph was unveiled in October 1919, with the Wolverton Prize Band in attendance. Four khaki-clad NCOs were mounted at each corner of the Cenotaph, resting on their arms reversed.

'For God, King and Country' – the North Bucks Branch of the Old Contemptibles Association dedicate their banner in the Park, Wolverton in the 1920s. The ceremony was attended by two military chaplains, and the standard-bearer was Charles R. Saggers.

Old Contemptibles, 'Chums' of 1914, at the laying-up of the standard, May 1971, in St George's Church where it is now kept. Left to right: Reg Hill, Dr E.D. Lawrence, Lieutenant-Colonel Dr A.H. Habgood, Charlie Saggers, Tom Stretton, Arthur Skerman, Tom Ferris. Others are Colonel Leslie Payne, Henry Durbridge and Mr J. Dundas.

After all the laughs and the splendid acting by the Wolverton St George's Players in 'Mother Goose' at the Church Institute, Wolverton 1949, the cast line up for the applause of their audience. Back row, left to right: -?-, Len Smallbones, Sid Dolling, Frank Brown, Bob Hunter, John McMillan, Iris Howe, Sidney Bolton, Bernard Harrison, Brian Brown, Walter Speaks, Lena Jakeman, Clifford Elliott, Ted Smallbones, Ted Robinson, Brian Camozzi. Second row: Rita Berridge, Pat Griffiths, Rosemary and Janet Fensome, John Stevens, Bill Coxhill, Roy Marsden, Fred Knight, Neil Dytham, Arthur Spong, -?-, -?-, Anita Lloyd, Jill and Jean Clarke. Third row, left side: Celia Holloway, ? Griffiths, Rosemary Carter, -?-, Jean Henson, -?-. Third row, right side: -?-, -?-, -?-, -?-, Sheila Owen, -?-. Front row: six unknown children, Mary Dormer, Yvonne Faux, Margaret Harrison (Principal girl), Joan Robinson (Principal boy), Mary Williams, Lesley Brown, -?-, -?-, -?-, Sheila Parrott, -?-. The producer was Revd Sidney Robert Bolton, curate, scenery was by Ken Speaks, while the dancing was provided by a troupe from Rosemary Carter's Dancing School.

Produced by the Curate of St George the Martyr, Wolverton, Revd Sidney R. Bolton, this is one of several annual nativity plays, 1947. In the left-hand group: Ben Henson, Charles Saggers, John Ranson, Arthur Spong, Mrs Percy Roberts, Sheila Parrott, Clifford Elliott, -?-. Front: -?-, 'Joseph', 'Mary'. Centre back: Revd Bolton (angel), Rose Elliott, Kathleen Speaks, Ken Speaks. In the right-hand group: Susan Crisp, Christine Speaks, Enid Tapp, Mrs May Harris, Maud Speaks. The church was built following the coming of the London & Birmingham Railway and was consecrated by the Lord Bishop of Lincoln on 28 May 1844. It celebrated its 150th anniversary in 1994.

The residents of Oxford Street, Wolverton, having won First Prize for the best decorated street, gather round the lovely cake to celebrate the Coronation of Queen Elizabeth II, 2 June 1953. Centre, left: Ted Cockerill; right: Reg Tite. Behind the table, near left-hand side: Kitty Tite with Brian. In front: Sandra Foxford, Jackie Tite, Kathryn Cockerill, Janice Savill. Behind right-hand side of table: Pauline Durdin. In front: David Durdin, Linda Mills, Gillian Gable.

Representing residents of Wolverton Urban District, Ted Cowley (aged 75), Frank Bates (74) and Bill Alderman (56) were first in the town pool at its official opening, 1 August 1964.

'Moustaches & Boaters': Jimmy Edwards, 'Three Men in a Boat' at the Empire Cinema, Wolverton, *c*. 1950. Included in the group are: Pete Held, Joe Jones, Ken Hooton, Gordon Parry, Mrs Jerham, Bill Pedley, Arthur Rice, Roy Jones, James Odell, Norman Brown, Bill Coxhill, Ken Speaks, Eric Swannell, Sid Swain, Ron Dee, Brian Barnes. In the immediate foreground is Monty Woollard's Lagonda 2-litre, built in 1927, taking part in a Toc H parade of cars.

Wolverton Girls' School (now Wyvern County First School), Aylesbury Street, Wolverton, *c.* 1934. Back row, left to right: Gladys West, Catherine Ager, Cecily Welford, Amy Stobie, Maud Dunkley, Gladys Smith, Joyce Davies, Lily Smallbones, Helen Marven, Cecily Stonebridge, Olive Wilson, Gwyneth Cooper. Middle row: Sylvia Robinson, Kathleen Lovell, Phyllis Pack, Margery Townsend, Margaret Jordon, Mary Axtell, Eunice Webb, Eileen Roberts, Joy Jerham, Kathleen Beech. Front row: Lena Jakeman, Edie Lucas, Irene Busby, Ethel Smith, Miss Doris Starmer-Smith (Headmistress), Dorothy Powell, Kathleen Tissington, -?-, Betty Henson. Sitting on ground: Cynthia Willis, Elsie Jones, Eileen Hobson, Violet Barton.

Wolverton Boys' School sports team, winners of the North Bucks School Athletics Trophy, 1931. Back row, left to right: Reg Adams, Fred Williams, Douglas Bagnall, Victor Espley, Bernard Reynolds, Douglas Norman, Cyril Mason, Victor Davis. Middle row: John Williams, Billy Coxhill, Mr B. Willett, Mr Herbert (Bert) Lunn (Headmaster, 1927–50), Mr C.H. Piper MC (Sportsmaster). Kneeling, left: Edward Brown. Right: John Hazell. Front row: Hubert Morris, Robert Merritt, Ronald Howe (with shield), Peter Briggs, John Lunn. From 1930–4 they succeeded in winning the North Bucks School Shield for Athletics and several boys took part in the County Sports, representing the school. For the school's enduring success in athletics, credit is due to Mr C.H. Piper MC, who was Sportsmaster for many years.

'The Bisto Kids': Gwyneth Cooper and Dorothy Snowdon took second prize in the fancy dress competition at the Wolverton Pageant in the mid-1930s.

The Wolverton Area Grand Carnival Parade and Gala Fête came into being in 1963 and was a popular annual event for fourteen years. In September 1968 the Radcliffe School Society entered this float, entitled 'Stone Age School'. Left to right: Peter Newcombe, Roger Haycock, Katie Horner (on bicycle), Michael Stock, June Savage, Tony Wood, Richard Burkett.

On Sunday afternoons in the 1920s, in the meadows by Haversham Bridge, one could watch keen young sportsmen motor-cycle racing, including Ron Page, Ray Sellick, Don Fortescue. Using HRDs (Harley Davidsons) and overhead-valve Nortons with sidecars (called 'chairs'), they competed all over the Midlands.

An action photograph from a match between Wolverton Town (white shirts) and Pinner Town, c. 1949. Left to right: Wilf Rose (centre forward), Charley Morley (inside left) Pete Hillyer (outside left). Note the crowd along the bank, on the least popular side. Gates were some three to four thousand.

Local Guides off to camp 1920s style, en route to Bow Brickhill in 1921 by horse and cart.

Their Annual Good Turn. Miss Sylvia Harnett and Miss Edith Walton (later Mrs H.E. Meacham), with Guides, cleaning the Wolverton War Memorial prior to the Remembrance Day Parade and Service, c. 1928.

The first girls in North Bucks to receive the Duke of Edinburgh's Gold Award were presented with their medals by Sir Frank Markham. Pam Walton, Jackie Tite and Pat Long of the Wolverton District Land Rangers, with Mrs Audrey Cooper (Captain), after receiving their certificates from the Duke of Edinburgh at Buckingham Palace, July 1967.

A rare photograph of one of the Wolverton and Stony Stratford steam trams; the Brush engine is here waiting in the loop with a full head of steam.

Queen Elizabeth II and Prince Philip visiting Warren Farm, Old Wolverton, 5 April 1966. On the left is Mr Ray Turney, in the centre, Mr Charles Turney. The Queen is talking to farmworkers John Mitchell and Robin Hewitt.

Mr Thomas Charles Turney came from Chicheley in 1918 to take the tenancy of Warren Farm. He moved across the road to Wolverton Mill in 1927, retiring eleven years later when the mill ceased working. He and his wife, Sarah Ann, are standing outside the Mill House, around 1935.

A tram returns to Stony Stratford; the lines to the depot can be seen on the left. Mr Walter Franklin's house, No. 23 Wolverton Road, is on the far side of the entrance. Originally operated by the Wolverton & Stony Stratford District Light Railways Company Limited, tram services commenced on 27 May 1887. Having changed its name several times, the company ran into financial difficulties and finally ceased operating after the General Strike in 1926. 'Our Tram', as it was affectionately called, had two conductors, one the famous 'Little Billy' (William Newton), and the other George Hawtin.

Acknowledgements

Knowing I was a life-long resident of Stony Stratford, David Watts of Bicester suggested that I might consider compiling this book and I extend my grateful thanks to him for introducing me to such a pleasurable activity during the past twelve months. I owe a debt of gratitude to my husband, Jim Lambert, for his patience and support, without which this publication would not have been possible. I am especially indebted to Robert Ayers, for agreeing to write the Introduction and for his excellent synopsis on the history of the area. The assistance of Ron Unwin, John Barnes and Ray Rowlson, who produced photographic copies, has ensured the inclusion of items from the collections of the Wolverton & District Archaeological Society, The Hanslope & District Society and W.E Wilyman, Chemist (glass plates). A special mention must go to Bill West, a local author who gave me access to his material, the Milton Keynes Museum of Industry and Rural Life for allowing research, and to Audrey Beardmore, Mary Rogers, Dorothy Ebbs, Phyllis Lovesy, Margery Norman, Bill Coxhill, Sir Gordon Roberts, George Dicks, William Henson, Peter Brazell and Don Hellings for their historical details and local knowledge.

Thanks are also due to the many people who have given their time and hospitality and willingly loaned their family photographs, scrapbooks and books of reference:

Brian Barnes • Albert Bass • Bill Beeton • Hannah Bird • Ernie Blow • Clive Boddington
Les Braggins • May Bright • Joan Brockway • Cyril Brown • Dorothea Burgess
Ann Burman • Rita and Alf Buswell • Canon Cavell-Northam • Mike Chappell
Sylvia Clarke • Nancy Colborne • Arthur Cowley • Enid Coxhill • Gladys Cropper
Edie Daniels • Gerald Ditum • Pam Egan • Rose Elliott • Ann Foddy • Larry Francis
Walter Franklin • Eva Gascoigne • George Gregory • Sybil and Bernard Groom
Ron Hall • John Haseldine • Irene Healey • Mary Henson • Mitch Hicks
George Higgs • Irene and Allen Holland • Malcolm Hooton • Evelyn Jaworski
Colin and Albert Kightley • Margaret and Alan Ladd • Olive and Ted Lambert
Les Lovesy • Ivy and Albert Nichols • Pat Price • Gladys Read • Anne Rowledge
Louie and Bill Rowledge • Mary Saggers • Gordon Sargent • Sylvia and Ken Sibthorp
Ann Stainsby • Sue Starr • Jean and John Starsmore • Gweneth Stock • Betty Sutton
Kitty Tite • Bobby and Tony Wain • Pam and John Webb • John Webster
Trevor Wells • Ann and Eric Westley • Reg Westley • Angela and Maurice Weston
Edna Wildman • Albert Willett (Australia) • Doris Willett (Whaddon) • Keith Wilyman
• David Wise • Mr F.M. Woollard • Carol Wray.

If I have inadvertently omitted anyone from the above list, I trust they will accept my sincere apologies.

Equally valuable has been the help of a number of people who put 'names to faces' on group photographs, thus providing as complete a record as possible.